BIGGER HEARTED

BIGGER HEARTED

A Retired Pediatrician's Prescriptions for Living a Happier Life

Ron Schneebaum, MD

Published by Thinking Heart Publishing
ISBN (paperback): 979-8-9917832-0-0
ISBN (ebook): 979-8-9917832-1-7

Book design and production by www.AuthorSuccess.com
Printed in the United States of America

To the many children I've cared for over the years
and to my wonderful daughters, Rachel and Rebecca,
who taught me so much about love.

Contents

Introduction

A large number of teenagers in my medical practice seemed to get along well with their parents. Their closeness differed from the usual media characterizations of family interactions, and I was curious about what made their connections work. To verify my impression, I asked these teens to pick a hero, someone they admired, and all of them chose their mother and father, except for one who selected Dr. Martin Luther King, Jr., when I said the person didn't have to be alive. I asked what worked in their relationships and received the perfect teenage answer: a shrug of the shoulders and, "I don't know."

When their parents joined us, I asked them the same question, and their responses were identical. I had to find the answer I was looking for on my own.

During wellness visits, I often asked parents to tell me their child's most valued qualities, the traits that will stand the test of time. In their responses, the parents of these teenagers gave me the answer I sought. It wasn't in what they said but in how they came to their comments. They looked at their children and seemed to read their responses off their faces and did so with eyes of admiration. These parents saw more in their children than these teens even appreciated in themselves, and that love builds bonds.

In contrast, I pictured the relationships between teenagers and their parents where such admiration and respect didn't exist. These teenagers would seek out their peers when they had questions or needed advice to avoid being misunderstood or put down by their parents.

Maria fell, hurt her arm, and came to my office. I didn't know this seventeen-year-old, as she usually saw one of my colleagues. She told me she had been to an obstetrician earlier that day. She was pregnant. She loved her boyfriend, and they looked forward to having the baby. She also hoped to finish high school and attend college. Telling her very religious and strict parents was Maria's biggest concern. She was worried that they wouldn't accept her or the baby. When I told Maria she could tell them at our office if that would help, she reassured me that she would be fine. Her arm wasn't broken, and she left.

I didn't see Maria again until her infant son, Anthony, came in for a visit when he was two months old. He was adorable, and Maria beamed with the warm smile of a loving mom. We talked about how she was doing. She told me that her parents supported her from the moment she told them she was pregnant and were better grandparents than she could have imagined. Love achieved its proper place.

According to Greek mythology, Prometheus took fire from the gods on Mount Olympus and gave it to humankind, paving the way for modern civilization. The fire he gave us is also the fire of love and courage, and it is seated in the human heart. Culture recognizes that love's home is in the heart through its art, by pointing to our hearts when we refer to love, and lately, through emojis of the heart.

The heart's love uplifts us and makes us feel whole, stronger, more alive, kinder, compassionate, and connected. It is a transcendent entity that spans cultures and time. It is visible in art worldwide and in the cultures of long ago. Far from being a lightweight, sentimental feeling, this love is as real as any physical object. Where a falling boulder would crush a stone, not feeling loved would just as assuredly crush the human psyche. Though it is invisible and cannot be weighed, measured, or tested in a lab, much of our lives revolve around seeking this love. It binds us as a people and connects us with nature.

This transcendent love lives within each of us; it lightens our load, fills us with life, and develops meaningful connections. We each have the ability to experience love, but whether we do so or not is our choice. This book offers numerous ways to welcome the presence and feel its power in our lives; it also helps us break down the barriers that prevent us from living with love in our daily existence.

Increasing our experience of love's warmth and strength differs from how we increase our material wealth. For the latter, we set our sights on what we want and develop plans for reaching it, whether it is a key on a shelf or a path to furthering our education. We cannot take hold of love in the same way, for it's not ours to take. Instead, we open to it, making space for it by working on ourselves, like we'd let more light into a room by opening the shades and cleaning the windows. As we connect with love and experience love in our thinking and actions, our hearts fill, and we feel strength, meaning, connection, and the enjoyment of life.

These pages not only detail ways to ignite love within our being but also offer ways we can become Prometheus-like, bringing the fire of love and courage into our relationships and activities. Its ideas are based on common sense and practical experience and require no particular belief system or practice. Every point has been thoroughly tested and applied. You put them directly into play, and you can test them yourself.

Each chapter, or *prescription*, sets the foundation for the next one, and each successive chapter sheds light on the ones before. Each chapter contains a list of reflections highlighting the ideas presented and a prescription at the end summarizing the chapter. The book's Addendum condenses the ideas in each chapter so they can be considered further.

As we become bigger-hearted by expanding the power and presence of love in our lives, we will be happier and live more meaningful lives. We can all do this.

PRESCRIPTION I

Thinking with the heart

My nephew's science class received a box of compasses; each student had one to set up. They placed the stem into its base, rested the indented center of the arrow onto its point, and let it balance. When they stepped back, they saw all the compasses pointing in the same direction. Our inner compass stands free when we place our hearts at our center and clear our minds from biases. This section details the steps to do this.

The Emergency Department sent Kim, a thirteen-year-old girl, to my office because she'd threatened suicide. The physician she saw determined that she wasn't an immediate threat to herself and sent her to my office for further treatment and follow-up. I hadn't met her before, and I was struck by how sweet she seemed and how nicely she and her mom spoke to each other. I wondered what had gotten Kim so upset that she'd threatened to kill herself, so I asked.

"I'm being bullied in school," she said.

"Is that the full problem?" I asked, thinking of other possible causes.

"Yes," she said. "It's some of the girls in my class."

I tried to ease her pain by offering insights about bullying based on my knowledge and experience. I told her that people who bully aren't happy themselves. Their home life must be terrible; otherwise, they wouldn't enjoy putting someone down. I told Kim about a time when I was bullied at her age. My family and I spent a month at a bungalow colony in the Catskill Mountains, a collection of cabins with a central meeting house. We arrived in August, and most other families had been there since the beginning of July. I spent the first night with kids my age, but after that, none of them would speak to me. They wouldn't even say hello when I passed them. I never knew what happened or why. I couldn't tell my parents, fearing that if I did, they'd get too involved. I spent most of that summer alone, and it wasn't fun.

I told her that bullying is a serious issue and that her school should protect students from it and stop it where it exists. I offered to write a note to the school, telling them what was going on, how much it bothered her, and that they had a responsibility to solve the problem. She liked that idea.

A question then came to my mind, though, one I'd never before considered:

"Is what they said about you true?" I asked. "No," she said.

"Are you sure? It's not about something important to you?" I asked.

"That's right. It isn't," she said, nodding her head.

"Ah, then," I said, "if their words aren't a direct attack on you, then they are an unpleasant nuisance that makes school uncomfortable. They aren't dangerous, and they can't hurt you. They invade your world like ants at a picnic. The ants can ruin the picnic and make it no fun, but they aren't a reason for hurting yourself."

She seemed to understand the difference I pointed out—between an attack and a merely disagreeable situation. After discussing this further, I excused myself to write a letter to her school. I read it to Kim and her mother, and they liked it.

Before our conversation, I thought I'd prescribe an anti-depressant, and I still offered her that possibility. She said she was okay without it, and her mother agreed. I told her to let me know if she changed her mind or wanted to get together again, and I thanked them for coming in.

The difference between a painful psychological attack and an unpleasant situation—the line of reasoning that changed how she felt about herself and about the words that were upsetting her—was a distinction I'd never made before. It arose as a spontaneous flash, fresh and direct. It was my idea, yet it spoke to her. It was a heart-based concept that originated through caring, seeing her problem, and seeking a solution.

Kim's story demonstrates that thinking with the heart and mind are two aspects of human cognition. Thinking with the heart begins with caring and compassion. Through this, we can see another's experience through their eyes and ask ourselves how we can support them and how we can help. Thinking with the mind is the term I use for brain-based, intellectual reasoning.

As I listened to Kim, for example, my mind reviewed all that I'd learned in medical school about bullying, depression, suicidal ideation, and modes of treatment. My heart's compassion tried to understand her experience, and I also thought of ways to support her. I let her know that she was right to be upset, that it was not her fault, and that adults should stop such bullying from happening. However, the thought that changed everything arrived through a route that parallels an optical phenomenon called an afterimage. When we stare at a color and then at a blank white wall, we won't see the original color. Instead, we will see its complement, its afterimage. Here, the answer came to me and addressed her concern. It was like an afterimage. That's how thinking with the heart works.

We regularly find such inspiration in the ordinary course of life. For example, if we were making lunch for children sledding on a winter day, we'd consider what we have on hand, live in their experience, and think about what would make a nice lunch after a morning out in the cold. When they eat what we prepared and hear their "yums," we feel good about our efforts, and our connections with them deepen.

Similarly, when business owners care about their customers' experiences, they feel good about their work. They're not just thinking about profits; they know their efforts add value to someone else's life.

Reflections

- When we think with the heart, we see through another person's eyes, consider how to support that person, and do this by imagining their perspective.
- Can you remember an instance where you thought with your heart?

Unlimited happiness

Many people think that we can't be *that* happy. This is based on a false notion, on a material view of happiness. If happiness is about getting that raise, a new job, or the perfect house, we can't be that happy because life only contains so many major events. In addition, the joy experienced from such events doesn't last. Once the novelty of a new item wears off, we revert to our earlier state of happiness. Our experience of happiness is limitless, but a different view of happiness is necessary to see this. The thought experiments Einstein used when he developed his theories of relativity can help. In one of them, he imagined riding on a beam of light, the fastest entity in the universe, and from that vantage point, he saw a different relationship between time and space. He formulated his thoughts into calculations, tested them, and they held.

Instead of riding on a beam of light, imagine riding on a beam of happiness. You can get onto this beam by remembering a time when you were happy or felt good about life, whether an isolated experience or something that occurs regularly. Let go of the event that carries the feeling and focus on the feeling. Scroll through your life and look for where else you've had that feeling. Group them into kinds. When I did this, I came up with the following short list:

- Experiencing love
- Rewarding relationships
- Activities I enjoy
- Being fully present
- Enjoying material things
- Sharing what I have with someone
- Helping others
- Striving toward a goal
- Having a sense of accomplishment
- Giving to others
- Experiencing gratefulness
- Feeling appreciated
- My sense of spiritual connection
- Knowing that we're loved

The list shows that material things make us happier, but a closer look is more nuanced. While we enjoy what we have, we also enjoy sharing. Therefore, a thing itself doesn't contain happiness. It's not like a container that holds a certain amount of liquid. If things contained happiness, we'd feel less happy if we gave what we had to someone else; even a present would do this because we'd have less. Things themselves don't bring happiness; our attitude towards them does. Two people could own the same thing, win the same prize, and get the same job, but that does not determine the amount of joy each finds in what they receive.

The Heart Is a Door to Connection

Sixteen-year-old Jermaine came to see me because he'd hurt his hand. It was swollen, and the side opposite his palm was black and blue. The bones hurt when I pressed them. He likely had a boxer's fracture, a broken bone from hitting a hard object. Girlfriends are almost always the reason for such injuries in teenage boys, and that was indeed the case here. Jermaine's girlfriend had broken up with him, and he tried to talk her out of it. She had none of it. Frustrated, he punched his locker. Besides caring for his hand, I wanted to help prevent him from doing this again and maybe even stop his friends from doing something similar. I told him he likely had a fracture and needed an x-ray. Thinking he'd ignore a lecture, I tried humor to frame the futility of his actions.

"So let me understand, Jermaine," I said. "You wanted your girlfriend back, so you punched your locker. Great plan, but it had problems: your hand isn't happy, your locker didn't care, and I'm not sure your ex-girlfriend thought, 'Wow! Jermaine punched his locker for me. Anyone who'll do that is my kind of guy. I'm going back with him.'"

He laughed and saw the pointlessness of his punch. Although we differed in age and background, the universal truth was the same. My thoughts could be helpful because we were just two people trying to figure out life. I could imagine his reality and speak from the universality of our hearts.

I liked DeShawn. He carried himself like a tough guy, but I thought he had a soft underbelly. At one visit, I gave this sixteen-year-old a pep talk about life to help him set his direction. I pointed out his positive qualities, telling him he had street smarts—a sense of people—and that many looked up to him. His leadership qualities, I reviewed, demonstrated a high level of intelligence, something very bright adults often don't have. I told him that life would bring challenges and that he would have to decide what kind of person he wants to be. If he didn't get distracted by drinking, drugs, and people who want to bring him down, he would not only succeed in life, but he would likely be able to do anything he wanted to, and he would mean a lot to people. He didn't look at me, but I knew he was listening. This became clear when a friend called, and he answered by saying, "I can't talk now. I'm chillin' with my doc."

Again, I could imagine DeShawn's experience using my heart and mind, and we could connect.

The Heart Is a Sense Organ

Before attending medical school, I worked for a newspaper representative firm, an advertising-related business, in midtown Manhattan and earned $12,000 a year. I found a three-room apartment in the fashionable Upper East Side for $159 a month. One day, I noticed that I felt off—emotionally, not physically—and couldn't figure out why. I sat on my couch and tried to figure this out. After closing my eyes, I called up this feeling of discomfort, and while I held it, I brought possible causes to mind, looking for a match for why I felt this way. I saw the reason: it was envy.

Beautiful buildings marked my neighborhood, some with

large, ornate lobbies, some with attendants in the front, and some charming, multi-level brownstones. Exclusive shops, expensive restaurants, and businesspeople wearing handsome three-piece suits were also prominent. I'd been unconsciously yearning to live that lifestyle and couldn't afford what they had. Once I knew the cause of my feeling down, I could think it through. I moved into the city knowing my entry-level salary wouldn't get me far. I wasn't even sure I wanted the lifestyle I found myself envying. My initial goal was to experience the city and enjoy its many inexpensive opportunities. I lived, for example, down the street from the Metropolitan Museum of Art, and Tuesday nights were free for me to enjoy. I had what I wanted and didn't need much else. As I reconnected with myself, this sense of envy melted away. I was whole again and was able to live my life.

The heart's inner sense of self adds to the five senses we learned about in school. Through it, we can feel our emotional state and sense its depth. Partnering this with our intellect allows us to look for the roots of our feelings, compare them to other times, and find possible ways out.

Our heart's sense also allows us to feel another person's inner state. While doing this, we can see how we can help. That was my approach when I saw Amar. When he came in for his adolescent wellness visit, Amar told me that his dad had been killed in a motorcycle accident. He was seventeen, an only child, lived with his mom, and only occasionally saw his father. Amar found out that his dad had a drinking problem through the accident, as his father's motorcycle spun out because he was drinking while driving it. He also learned that his dad's drinking led to his parents' divorce. The accident occurred while Amar's father was visiting his parents in Albania. The family blamed Amar's mom for his drinking, as no one else in their family had a problem with alcohol. Amar's mom, who was in the room with us, denied having alcohol issues, adding that her not drinking did not stop them from blaming her. She felt it stemmed from their leftover anger over his marrying her. When they divorced, they cut her off from contact with them. And they cut off Amar after the accident—they wouldn't talk to him about what happened, and they wouldn't let him visit. Besides the pain from the loss, he wanted to see the site of the accident and talk with his dad's family. He also suffered from guilt, feeling he could have been a better son. Amar's eyes filled with tears as he told me his story.

He wouldn't see a psychiatrist or a therapist, he refused to take antidepressant medication, and he denied thoughts of self-harm. I became his de facto mental health provider. He and his mom were close; she often stayed in the room during our conversations, and she felt she could monitor his psychological state.

We spoke in depth about his father's death, his feelings of guilt, the normalcy of mourning, and the problems with trying to get someone to stop drinking. I told Amar that he could not have prevented his father's drinking, even if he'd known about it. I pointed out that even his mother couldn't affect this change. His mom backed me up.

I suggested that he and his mom hold a memorial for his dad as a way to gain closure. I knew this would be hard for his mom to do, as it would likely trigger many of her own feelings about her ex-husband. I let Amar know how difficult this would be for her. He understood, and she agreed to the idea. I saw him again several weeks later. They'd held a memorial. It not only helped him; seeing his mom's willingness to help also meant a lot.

I saw Amar several more times, and we continued to discuss the normalcy of mourning and how he could not have been any different as a son than he was. Part of his lack of closeness with his dad, I reassured him, had to do with his dad's issues.

At one of our visits, Amar told me that he had been having difficulty with schoolwork since the accident. I told him that his dad would have wanted him to do well in school, and he would not have wanted his death to be the reason for his son's failure to do so. I suggested that Amar dedicate his schoolwork to his dad and put a picture of him on his desk. He later told me that this helped.

To follow his progress and ensure his healing and safety, I combined what I had learned from my training and experience with objective testing, his reporting, his mom's comments, and my sense of his self.

Once, one of my daughters had a friend over. They were five years old, and they got into a clash with each other. They were upset, didn't want to play anymore, and came to tell me about it. Using this same sense of self, I felt their problem wasn't deep, and I developed a plan based on that. I told them to stand back-to-back, one against the other, and said this in a serious, but not scary, voice. When they were in position, I said, "Okay. Now wiggle."

While wiggling, they bumped into each other and cracked up. That was it. They went back to playing as if nothing had happened.

Following Our Inner Light

We also have an inner sense of light to help us plan our actions. A new developmental screening program was being rolled out in my office, and I didn't like it. I thought it might needlessly worry parents and not offer many benefits. I spoke to the heads of my department, as they were the ones behind our implementation, and learned that the American Academy of Pediatrics had developed it. My department heads, therefore, were not going to decide against it. We were meeting to discuss its implementation, and I had to think about what I would say at the meeting. Our medical assistants would hand out and score the screening questionnaires when the project launched. They liked me and trusted my opinions. I would only create conflict if I spoke against the program, and the program would be implemented anyway. As I considered my options, I looked at my sense of inner light, and it shined most brightly when I entertained the idea of giving the rollout my full backing. The new program was going into effect anyway, and supporting it and the staff would enhance departmental harmony. Looking back, I was so glad that I took this approach. It was the right one.

Business recommends using this sense of light when receiving an upsetting email. Instead of immediately responding, it suggests pausing to reflect on how you will feel about it later. Looking for light when deciding on our actions is part of living happily and strengthening relationships.

Reflections

- Have you used your sense of self to assess your mental state?
- Have you used this sense to find ways out of your current issues?
- Have you used it to sense another and to chart your course?
- Have you used your sense of inner light to guide your actions?

The Heart as a Listener

Listening has unexpected power. If we have a problem, a friend's attentive ear can help us feel better, even without them saying anything. Such listening parallels the process of a boat traveling through a canal. Canals connect bodies of water that are at different levels. The boat enters a chamber called a lock. The doors in front and behind it close, and the water level of the two locks is raised or lowered until their heights are the same. The gate opens, the boat passes to the next lock, and the process continues until it travels the canal.

Attentive listening similarly gets people onto the same level. It is a sacrificial act, for the listener puts aside other thoughts. The process is healing because the boat traveling from one to the other is love, and love heals and connects. Through this space, one can also achieve insights about what to say or do in any situation.

Such listening is not always easy. My grandmother taught me this and the value of going through the discomforts that might arise. She'd immigrated from Europe to the US between the two World Wars, hadn't been married, was an only child, and had no relatives in the US. She met my grandfather a few years after his wife, the mother of his three children, had died. His children were married and living on their own at the time. When my grandfather was in his late eighties, they moved from the Bronx to a newly built apartment complex in Queens, one of New York's other boroughs. He died a few years later. She couldn't stand straight because of unusually weak muscles and got around by leaning over her walker and shuffling her feet.

My parents, aunts, and uncles visited her regularly after my grandfather's death, even though they had no real connection to her. She was the only grandmother I ever knew. My grandmother was not an easy lady. "How could you wear that tie with that shirt?" was her greeting to one of my uncles when he visited. Another uncle tried to cheer her up by pointing out her beautiful view. I saw that his attempt to make her feel better completely missed the mark.

She was also a challenging conversationalist. If I telephoned and began conversations with, "How are you, Grandma?" she usually answered, "Like an old lady. How could I be?"

If I started with, "What's new, Grandma?" she'd answer, "Oy.

What could be new?"

I decided to befriend her when I was in college. I had a car, and we both lived in Queens. I drove her to doctor appointments, painted her kitchen with a friend, and, one day, brought Chinese food for us to have for dinner.

While taking our food out of its white boxes and putting it onto plates, I remembered my uncle's failed attempt at making her feel better and decided to take a different tack. I'd try to understand her reality and how she dealt with her physical problems. "Your life is so hard, Grandma. How do you manage?" I asked as we ate. After she answered, I asked about some of the specifics of what she told me. I was interested in and wanted to understand her experience. We went on like this for a while, and then she looked at me with a sparkle in her eyes and said, "Enough about me. How are you?"

And then we had the most beautiful back-and-forth conversation for the rest of our dinner.

I took a leap of faith when I asked about her difficulties; I had no idea what to expect. I listened and asked questions only to understand her better. This was a purely human interaction. The heart's loving compassion brought us together, and the interaction enriched each of us.

Listening also includes holding back from reflexively trying to make things better. A friend of mine was a hospital-based doctor during the early phase of the AIDS epidemic in the South Bronx. The disease was not understood then, and medicines hadn't been developed to treat it. One of his patients, Ms. Webster, had AIDS and had been admitted because of a severe cough, fever, and poor oxygenation. She was known to the nurses and staff because she had been hospitalized before. During this hospitalization, however, she was hostile toward her caregivers, used aggressive language, made threats, and almost became physically combative. This was not like the woman they knew. The staff asked him to talk with her. When he reviewed Ms. Webster's chart before going to see her, he noted that she had been diagnosed with pneumocystis carinii pneumonia. This infection was known to be a death sentence, as there was no treatment for it at the time.

When he went into the room to talk with her, she told him that she had just found out that she had pneumocystis, and it was clear that was the reason for her personality change. He didn't know what to do, as his medical training didn't teach physicians how to act in such situations. And then he remembered the words of a favorite medical school professor: "Don't just do something; sit there."

He stayed, they talked, Ms. Webster cried, and they talked more. This exchange allowed her to vent and begin grappling with what she'd learned. Now, she could start talking about her diagnosis, her thoughts, and her plans.

Depending on our backgrounds, we might naturally want to protect ourselves from feeling the pain of others, just as our eyes spontaneously blink when something threatens to enter them. Still, we can listen, feel their difficulties, and be present. And we can do this without taking their problems with us. We don't have the problem; they do. We can be there with them, listen, and help them by being present, but we don't have to take their hurts with us. Being with another through their challenges builds enriching bonds.

During morning rounds in the nursery, another pediatrician and I were paged to the emergency department. There had been a tragic car accident, and one of the passengers was a child. After an unsuccessful attempt at resuscitation, I spent time with the family. Then, I had to go to my office to greet my first patient, Tracy, who was celebrating her fifth birthday. During the ten-minute drive, I had to drop everything that had happened so that I could be fresh for Tracy.

The steps I used are the same as the ones we can all use when listening to someone going through a difficult time. I began by appreciating that I couldn't take events that occurred to others personally. Numerous fatal car accidents were happening across the globe. I was involved in this one and did all I could. I had to leave without taking the emergency department events with me. I would wear down emotionally if I couldn't do this, and it would also affect my other relationships.

I could let go by assessing these events with my heart and mind. I used my medical skills as best I could and was fully engaged when I was with the family. I actually felt good about the care I delivered and was ready to meet what was next and move on from it.

In the same way, you can listen to a friend's concerns with an open mind and be fully present. Then, you can close the door, feeling good about having listened and reminding yourself of the value of a friend.

In medicine, we also do one other thing that is helpful in letting go: we don't gossip about patients and our interactions with them. In fact, it's against the law. This allows us to drop what happened and not carry it with us. If I talked about it with friends at the office and at home, the memory would continue to live on in my mind.

Reflections

- Has anyone ever listened to you in the way described?
- Have you ever listened to anyone in the way described?
- Was it beneficial?

Serving Love

I was visiting friends and joined them when they went to their neighbor's house to celebrate their son's first birthday. I soon wondered what I would do at this barbecue. I had little in common with most of the adults there; their children were in daycare with the birthday boy, and my daughters were in high school. After some introductory hellos and friendly chats, I spotted a tray of meat and vegetables in the kitchen. "I've got the grill," I said, imagining that the hosts, who would be doing the grilling, would rather be with their friends.

The barbecue grill was set up in an alcove outside. While the guests were inside, I enjoyed cooking and liked seeing the food plates returning empty. I was glad that I could contribute. I didn't have to do this. If I had gotten into an interesting conversation, I could have continued it. The hosts just wanted their guests to have a good time. Living with our hearts as a guide positions us to see choices that make us feel good, which we might not have otherwise noticed.

Thinking with heart and mind also applies to the workplace, where we can inwardly ask what we can do that would be helpful.

During the COVID pandemic, the head of a local mental health center thought about the psychological toll working from home might be taking on his staff. They not only had to practice in a way they weren't trained for, but he also wondered about how the lack of in-office camaraderie might have affected them. To find out how they were doing, he called each of them during their working hours, staying up late for several nights so he could talk to those who covered late-night emergencies. His actions represent a practical translation of one's heartfelt concerns for the staff at his workplace. When we act from the heart, we feel better, and it's our choice.

Having a Strong Ego vs Being Egoless

We can have a strong ego and still be centered in our hearts. Success in a career requires a strong ego, and we appreciate the expertise of such a person. We go to the best surgeons, read books by acclaimed writers, attend concerts by accomplished musicians, watch top athletes, and wish to have excellent teachers for our children. In addition, I have always tried to be the best pediatrician I could be.

How can we have the strong ego needed to strive to be excellent at whatever we do and simultaneously be on a heart-centered path? Goethe, the poet and scientist, provided a possible way in one of his poems, *Die into Becoming*. This phrase tells us that we can be great, as great as we can be, in whatever we do. However, when we step outside of the area of our expertise, we can drop this sense of greatness and just be a fellow human being.

Children force this on caring adults. Imagine that you are the best at whatever you do, receive all the praise and monetary rewards that come with this level of excellence, and come home to your smiling six-month-old, to your toddler who wants to play with you, or to your teenager who is concerned about something and wants to talk; nothing of what you do in your workplace counts at that moment.

Being present means dropping the cloak of whatever stature you carry and being with them as if nothing else in the world is as important. Die—drop any sense of superiority—and become a complete human being, ready for what your next relationship asks of you. And you can do this if you are centered in your heart. Follow your passions, enjoy your interests and pursuits, and strive to be great at what you do, but don't define yourself by your accomplishments or stature.

Gratefulness

Our hearts are the home of gratitude; gratefulness fills us whenever our hearts open to love. Two brief exercises can help generate a sense of gratitude. Doing them once can have lasting effects. I invite you to try them:

Consider an article of clothing you own and think of everyone involved in getting it to you: the people who packed it, shipped it, and delivered it; the cars, trucks, and planes involved; the farmers, road builders, and miners who dug out the needed raw materials; and the researchers who designed the machines that made these products. Think of all the people involved in feeding these workers, their families, and the pets that keep them happy. Carry this out as far as possible and see how far it goes. Appreciating everyone who made it possible to have my clothing, including those who put in long hours or worked under challenging conditions, brings waves of thankfulness and appreciation.

Fill yourself with gratitude the next time you buy food at a supermarket. Live with this from the moment you walk through the door until you exit, and don't let any negative thoughts enter your mind. Live in gratefulness as you pass the fresh fruits, vegetables, meats, fish, dairy products, frozen goods, and wide-ranging packaged items. Appreciate that you did nothing directly to achieve all this, and yet it is there for you.

The first exercise can take a few minutes, and the second lasts as long as you are in the store. Both can have powerful effects, so don't just read them; spend time with them. They can drive home the appreciation that our lives depend on the contributions of others, including the gifts the natural world brings us. The after-image of the gratitude that develops is a desire to give back, to take our turn contributing in whatever way we do.

Living in Flow

Being fully present in an activity defines a state referred to as *flow*. During such times, we are one with what we are doing. All our knowledge and experience go into these situations; though we have nothing on our minds at such times, we are at our best. Athletes call this *being in the zone*. Baseball hitters say the ball seems to slow down and get bigger at such times. Abraham Maslow called these *peak experience*s and saw them as life's best times. Mihaly Csikszentmihalyi, one of the chief researchers into the flow state and the person who coined the term, noted that getting into the flow state requires a person to have three things: a difficult challenge, the skills to meet it, and an interest in doing so.

Csikszentmihalyi puzzled over how we could fall into the flow state more regularly. While he saw the value in such times, he also noticed that many people don't even have one activity that regularly puts them into the flow state; very few have more than one. Maslow couldn't take this further; he felt that peak experiences usually only happen when we are doing something we thoroughly enjoy.

Being bigger hearted allows us to live in a flow state regularly. We are fully present, listening, and pondering how to support them. This state of being in flow adds another dimension to being happier.

The Power and Nature of Love

I have enjoyed a wide range of spiritual and religious practices and readings, including Black Elk, an Ogalala Sioux holy man; George Washington Carver, a devout Christian; Martin Buber, a Jewish mystic and philosopher; Rudolf Steiner, a seer, scientist, and educator; the Gospels; and the Bhagavad Gita. Each touched my heart in the same way, and it was also the same locale where I experienced love. This made me wonder whether love was the force behind the traditions I knew. If it were, I would need no other religious/spiritual practice to connect me with that divine energy. I wanted to test this idea, and I thought of one way to do so: I would drop all of my other practices—the holidays I celebrated, the readings I did, and the uplifting podcasts and other social media channels that touched on spirituality—and only follow love, my heart's sense of compassion and caring, and I would see if the inner connections I had developed diminished because I had eliminated my spiritual/religious practices. If it did, I'd look to see which was the missing piece, the practice that cut me off from my feeling inwardly connected. I would then put that back into my repertoire.

I was not hoping for a particular outcome and spent more than two years engaged in this test. My results were unequivocal: following love—seeking to follow the heart—was a complete spiritual path. This could only be the case if Love were behind the veil and was that same entity referred to as God, Inner Light, Divine Energy, Christ, or Allah, and was also the reality behind nature.

Following written tradition, I will capitalize Love when it's used as the name of the divine. I will use many terms for this entity to show that I am not speaking from a specific tradition; I am referring to a universal entity. Where I use God, Love, or Divine Energy, please use whatever term works for you.

Reflections

- Can you see how a strong ego and inner connectedness are entirely compatible?
- How differently would you act if you felt that a piece of the heavenly lived within?
- How differently would you treat others if you thought that a piece of the heavenly lived within?

Self-Care

This section reviews my five—to ten-minute morning routine. I do this before I open my eyes. If you use an alarm clock, set it to include this time. When you turn it off, don't look at notifications or messages; simply close your eyes. First, fill yourself with love. There are several ways to do this; one isn't better.

- Remember a time when you felt loved, and fill yourself with that feeling.
- Remember that a piece of the Heavenly lives within and feel that experience.
- Rekindle the feeling brought by a favorite verse or prayer and fill yourself with that.

I let the experience of love fill my heart and radiate outward (I will discuss this in more detail in the last chapter). I then review my upcoming day in three different ways. The first is a quick helicopter view to give me a general sense of what I will be doing, the second looks at the details more closely, and the third explores *how* I want to be. An example of this routine follows, using an imaginary day from earlier in my life.

1. When I finish my review, I'll say hello to Andrea, prepare for the day, greet the kids, have breakfast, and go to work. After work, I'll go to the gym, come home, have dinner, spend time with my family, and sleep.

2. I look through the upcoming day, focusing on specific details.

   Andrea is leaving early. I will be making breakfast and driving the kids to school. I'll make oatmeal for breakfast, and we also have bagels. The kids' lunches are in the fridge. They'll gather what they need for school. I'm going to the dry cleaners this morning and must remember to take the laundry bag. I'll see patients, then we have a lunchtime meeting, so I won't need to bring lunch. I'll then see my afternoon patients. I'm going to the gym after work; my gym bag is in the closet, and I need to take extra socks. I'll be home for dinner after the gym, hang out, put the kids to bed, and Andrea and I will have some time together before we go to sleep.

3. I do one more review to explore how I want to **be** during the day.

Since I have the kids, I will get up early. I don't want to feel rushed when I'm with them. I'll spend time picturing the mood I'd like to create at breakfast and the mood I want to achieve in the car. Since I'm with the kids, I'll look at my emails and messages after I drop them off. I'll close my eyes before leaving my car at the office and ask Love to join me. I'll think about the folks I work with and consider whether there is anything I can say to anyone that will be helpful. This could include thanking my medical assistant for helping us get through a busy, crazy day the day before, thinking of a story one of my colleagues might like, or telling them something about one of their patients I saw the day before. I'll briefly review our lunchtime meeting and how I want to carry myself. If there are complicating factors, I'll review the meeting later in the morning. When I get home, I'll pause to fill myself with Love before entering the house.

I find multiple benefits with this morning routine:

- Stress reduction: I see that I will get through the day.
- I remember details I might have otherwise forgotten.
- I can think about how I wish to act.
- Filling myself with Love is nourishing, and it sets my direction.

I also review the day before I fall asleep in the evening. After closing my eyes and just before I fall asleep in the evening, I fill myself with Love and then review the day going backward, starting at bedtime and finishing in the morning. This is a helicopter view that only looks at highlights. I want to see what worked, what didn't, and what I can learn. I close this out by looking for the miracles that might have occurred during the day—the small things that make my hair stand on end and let me know I'm not alone. I then fill myself with Love and go to sleep.

I will review this routine again at the beginning of the last chapter so my description will be clear enough for you to try it out.

Prescription

- If our team had an upcoming match, our theater ensemble was taking on a new play, or if we were presenting a project at work, we'd prepare for it.
- Do the same for your upcoming day.

The next prescription is for healing our inner hurts, particularly the ones from childhood.

PRESCRIPTION II

Healing Childhood Hurts

Three-year-old Wayne tripped over a boulder while running and fell. Unhurt, he got up, brushed himself off, went back to the boulder, and kicked it for getting in his way. Blaming yourself for your childhood trauma is as futile. This next section details how to heal these childhood hurts and reconnect with love.

According to an old legend, a lion's paw had a splinter, and it caused the lion a lot of pain. Over time, the splinter became infected. Stepping on it was excruciating. The lion didn't know the cause of this discomfort, but it left him constantly on edge and angry. He swatted at anything that came near; he just wasn't himself. A mouse, who saw the splinter and recognized it as the source of the lion's pain, snuck up to the lion, tugged at the splinter, and pulled it out. The pus drained, the pain subsided, the wound healed, and the mouse and the lion became best friends.

Our childhood hurts are that splinter. They affect how we see ourselves and how we see the world. Pulling them out begins the path to healing.

Naomi, age fifteen, was depressed and anxious. An only child, she lived with her dad, her grandmother, and her grandmother's boyfriend. Naomi's mom, battling drugs and psychological pain, left the family when Naomi was a toddler. Her dad traveled for work, leaving Naomi with her grandmother and her partner. The older couple made fun of Naomi, called her names, and told her that she'd never amount to anything, and they yelled at her, especially when they drank. Her dad knew that he should have asked his mother and her boyfriend to leave, but he felt guilty about doing so; she had promised that they would stop drinking, and he also couldn't afford to lose their childcare.

Naomi's anxiety and depression originated in her difficult life circumstances, and these exemplify what are termed Adverse Childhood Events (ACEs). These almost universal childhood insults affect psychological well-being.

Jaxson's mother brought him in because she was worried about his anger. I asked what upset him; he seemed like a nice guy. "I don't like it when people get in my face or bother me," he replied.

I pointed out that he'd gotten into trouble for fighting in school and that his anger would have more severe consequences if it continued. Our conversation helped him, but its effect didn't last long. He came in a few more times to discuss the topic. At one of these visits, the origins of his anger became apparent: his dad was mean to his mom, he yelled a lot, and his dad even came close to hitting her.

This upset Jaxson, triggering his anger and making him feel out of sorts.

The effects of ACEs often last for a person's entire lifetime. My mother's experience first taught me about this. She was the youngest of seven children born into a poor Russian family that immigrated to the Bronx, one of New York City's five boroughs after World War I. Her father died when she was five. The five girls shared one bedroom, the two boys the other, and my grandmother slept on the living room couch. She sold newspapers near the entrance of a subway station to bring in the needed cash to feed her seven children. On cold winter days, she wrapped her feet in extra newspapers and sidled to the subway grates to catch wafts of warm air from the station below whenever possible. She worked long hours, and my mother's older sisters mostly raised her. My mom also told me that her mother wasn't very caring; she even thought her mother was somewhat mentally challenged. This combination—her mother not being around and the lack of love she felt coming from her—caused my mother to think that she was unloved, and this came with the feeling that she was unlovable. A deep-seated sense of insecurity and a desire to be loved grew within, and she carried this with her for the rest of her life.

We can heal these hurts without opening to their pain, and we can do so on our own. Start by taking a psychological inventory. Go through the following list of common ACEs and note the ones you lived through. You do not have to reexperience what happened.

- **Challenging Environments**
  - Homes where children were neglected, mistreated, felt underappreciated or unloved
  - Homes with yelling, fighting, and abusive language
  - Homes where the effects of drugs or alcohol dominated, where severe emotional or mental health issues were a part of everyday life
  - Living in extreme poverty or an unsafe neighborhood
  - Being bullied

- **Loss**
  - The loss of someone important, either through their death or because they left the family

- **Bodily abuse**
  - Physical trauma or sexual abuse

- **Prejudice**
  - Racial bigotry
  - Sexual discrimination
  - Cultural or socioeconomic biases

- Some grew up with solid, loving parents with demanding expectations, but sometimes, these expectations went against their children's strengths and styles.

Childhood Hurts Go Beyond the Injury

Children who faced challenging lives were not at fault for what happened, but their young psyches could only make sense of these events by blaming themselves for what happened and believing the negative things said about them. This was buried in their unconscious and became the filter through which they see themselves and the world. These events can be buried so deeply that some adults don't even remember their abuse. Instead, they feel unexplained sadness, anxiety, depression, and anger without knowing why.

These destructive aspects of a child's psyche are untaught. Maria was convinced that she had murdered her mother. She was eight years old, her mother was dying of cancer, and the two of them lived with her mother's sister and brother-in-law. Maria's dad had never been a part of their life. Her mother was bedridden, and Maria spent every spare moment in a chair at her mother's bedside, surrounding her with her love. One evening, while perched in her usual spot, she overheard her aunt and uncle talking in the kitchen.

"Flo," her uncle said, "Let's move to California when this ends. We could buy a house and maybe live near the ocean."

"That would be wonderful," her aunt replied.

Knowing that she'd live with her aunt and uncle when her mother died, Maria imagined living in a big house by the ocean with a dog and running along the waves. That night, she fell asleep happy for the first time in a long time. At the same time, her mother had slipped into a coma, didn't wake up that next morning, and died in the afternoon. Maria was convinced that by abandoning her—thinking about having fun instead of protecting her mother with loving thoughts—she had killed her.

She did live with her aunt and uncle, but they never moved, and they treated her like a second-class member of the house, a treatment she felt she deserved for what she had done. She worked hard in school and was nearing the end of her Ph.D. when she felt her buried inner pain, and her world collapsed. The horrors of the past pressed in on her. She couldn't cope, dropped out of school, and dove into drinking and drugs, catching odd jobs along the way. She had fallen out of multiple relationships, and it wasn't until she was in her fifties that she met someone who truly loved her. Through this, she developed a strong enough sense of self to go to a therapist for the first time, where she made real progress.

Children respond to their childhood hurts in varied ways:

1. A few get through virtually unscathed.

During his annual well-child visit, Lyle, a ninth-grader, casually mentioned that he lived with his aunt and uncle; his father had died from a drug overdose, and his mother was in jail for dealing drugs. He seemed likable, friendly, and upbeat, and he was also a good student. I told him I was impressed; most people with his life story would get dragged down by his parents' lives, and that seemingly hadn't happened with him. He agreed that he was doing well, and I asked how he did it. "I saw what happened to them," he said, "and I decided I wouldn't let that happen to me."

2. The trauma can affect one's mental stability and sense of self.

Naomi walked on eggshells, not wanting to upset the older couple. Sometimes, they were pleasant when they drank, and sometimes they were cruel. Besides depression, she developed anxiety from this instability.

3. Some lose their sense of well-being.

A woman who ran a major tennis center in Florida was returning from an inpatient drug and alcohol rehab facility when I met her. She had the perfect career, she told me, but her past had been too much for her to manage. Her parents drank a lot, and when they did, they often told her that she was worthless and that they wished they'd never had her. She knew she had to leave the house and saw a tennis scholarship as the way. Her hard work in school and at her game got her a college scholarship. After graduation, she toured as a pro and developed the center.

Everything was going well until she had a boyfriend who drank a lot. She joined him, and they often drank too much. The barriers she'd erected to keep back the horrors of her past broke down, and she once again saw herself as worthless—hurts that went so deep only drugs and drinking could numb her pain.

4. These memories can affect relationships.

Jaxson didn't like how his dad treated his mom. He worried about her, which produced a state of anger and rage that would likely continue, particularly when people he was close to upset him. Without healing, he wouldn't be able to see that his actions were precisely what he desperately fought against.

5. Unhealed trauma can erode trust and lead to self-loathing.
Children who are sexually abused are often repeatedly preyed upon by people they should have trusted. The threats and cajoling tactics of their perpetrators lead them to believe they are somehow responsible for these horrible acts. They feel ashamed for having participated in their abuse, and they can't tell anyone.

6. Sometimes, the things parents do to encourage a child can backfire and negatively affect self-confidence.
I've known children whose loving parents tried to give them an extra boost, thinking a kickstart would help them take off. John, who was shy, was encouraged to make friends with the 'socially popular' kids. Marion's parents got too involved in her life. Whenever she expressed interest in an activity, they'd try to fan its flames and make a big deal about it. Mark attended schools with special programs as his parents tried to boost his lagging academics. These children sensed what their parents felt: they weren't good enough as they were, and the activities they were pushed into made them feel worse because they weren't the right fit.

7. Unhealed traumas can lead to abusive relationships.
Children who experience ACEs often find themselves in abusive relationships in later life. The nature of these

relationships parallels their earlier treatment, and they likely don't value themselves enough to demand more.

8. ACEs can also affect intimacy.
A child who doesn't feel loved will have difficulty expressing love, and those people who were sexually abused face enormous challenges.

The Roots of Healing

We can heal, and if we do, then the path takes two different directions:

- We can stop feeling responsible for our childhood hurts and believing that what was said about us was true.
- We can learn to connect with and fill ourselves with love.

The power in these false thoughts becomes clear if we imagine the children described hadn't blamed themselves and didn't see themselves as unlovable. If my mother didn't feel my grandmother's actions were a sign of her being unworthy of love, her outer life would have been the same, but she would have experienced it differently. She would not have developed the insecurity that caused her so much pain, and without this, she would have been a different spouse, mother, friend, schoolteacher, and grandmother. The tennis pro might have worked just as hard to get out of her oppressive house, but she would not have seen herself at fault for her parents' mean and drunken tirades. She would have enjoyed her dream job and love for the game without ghosts from her past threatening to peek through. Drinking would not have had the same hold on her, and she would have thoroughly enjoyed her life. The death of my friend's mother would have still hurt, but she would not have shouldered the pain of thinking she had done something wrong. Her aunt and uncle would have still abused her, but she would have known that what they did was wrong. She might have become a leader in the field of child advocacy, she could have gone to medical school to help in the fight against cancer, or she could have enjoyed her family with a life marked by deep and rewarding relationships.

A story from Greek mythology presents a way to heal. Theseus battled the Minotaur, a monster trapped deep within a highly complicated maze—a labyrinth. He took on the challenge because the Minotaur had been causing great devastation. Armed with a sword for his battle, Ariadne, his lover, gave him a ball of thread and told him to unravel it as he went through the maze. He defeated the Minotaur and followed Ariadne's string to find his way back to the light of day.

If the Minotaur represents the devastation caused by our childhood traumas, the labyrinth is the unconscious, where these false thoughts reside and wreak havoc on our psyches. The sword is the knowledge that we weren't at fault for what happened to us. Theseus used that sword to destroy the Minotaur and free himself from its controlling devastation. Besides getting out, we need to fill ourselves with the love we missed. The string Ariadne gave him, the healing power of love, allowed him to find the warm light of sunshine.

The first step in healing is to see that what happened to us was not our fault. Even if we were challenging to raise, these were our primary caregivers, and we deserved better. The second part is to see that we are loved and lovable.

Seeing others as the cause of our problems is not about blaming them or making ourselves victims; it is establishing the clarity we need to walk away from the lies we've held onto for so long. The following groups the insults we faced with the thoughts that can begin to free us from the grips of past events.

For all who experienced ACEs:

- The bad things that happened to us weren't our fault
- The negative things said about us weren't true
- The adults who cared for us should have known and done better

For people who have experienced challenging home environments:

- You deserved a safe, supportive, and loving environment
- You deserved to be loved for who you were and as you were
- Not receiving love was not your fault

For people who faced loss:

- The loss in your life was sad, but it wasn't your fault
- You could not have prevented another's death
- You could not have stopped someone from leaving
- You are not the reason someone drank or abused drugs
- You could not have stopped someone's drinking or drug use

For people who were sexually and/or physically abused:

- What your attacker did is immoral and illegal
- What your attacker did was shameful
- What happened was not your fault
- Your actions did not encourage them
- Adults should have restraint and act like adults
- The person who abused you likely abused others
- You could not speak up because you were a child; you were threatened, and you were scared
- You can let go of feeling guilty about what happened to others

For people who faced prejudice:

- I cannot suggest how you face the burden of prejudice, but I hope the ideas here can help you build a path to wholeness

Focused Inner Listening

Andrea and I rented a house after we married. I wanted to plant a garden, and the owner said I could use the land where an old shed stood. After taking down the structure, I smashed its concrete base, removed it, and added topsoil. This effort turned into a beautiful and plentiful garden and parallels the work of our changing thought patterns and rebuilding how we see ourselves. Just knowing that our caregivers didn't provide a nurturing environment or harmed us is usually not enough to change our feelings about ourselves and the world. Our psychological structure has to be taken down, the light-blocking ideas about ourselves removed, and new soil of rich concepts added. A healthy sense of self can then grow into fruition. I call the process Focused Inner Listening. It consists of six different tools, including:

- Constant pondering
- Thinking while lying in bed
- Journaling
- Taking long walks
- Talking with a friend
- Working with a mental health professional

I will use the idea that what happened to you wasn't your fault to highlight how you can work with these tools.

- **Constant pondering:** Spend free time reviewing the idea that what happened to you wasn't your fault. Consider this while showering, doing chores, or driving alone. We were children and had nothing to do with the conditions in our homes.

- **Think while lying in bed:** When you are in bed with your eyes closed, go over the idea that your childhood circumstances weren't your fault. Continue until you are tired, and then go to sleep.

- **Journaling:** Hold written dialogues with your caregivers, asking them why they behaved as they did. Write about the idea that how you were treated was not your fault. Free yourself from what happened. Use pen and paper or a computer. The journals can be kept, but that's not necessary. The ideas you work with are what count, not the record.

- **Take long walks:** During long walks, consider how you should have been raised. Think about how your experience affected your self-image and your life. Recognize that you were not at fault for what happened. Talk to yourself if that helps you stay focused. If the area is secluded enough, scream at those who hurt you. Ask them why they didn't take better care of you. Crying is okay. Venting can help release self-blame. Let go of the hurts they caused.

- **Work with a mental health professional:** A mental health professional might help you go deeper than you can alone. The work here differs from traditional forms of therapy. Find someone willing to work with you.

- **Talk with a friend:** Talk with a friend about your insights and progress. This could especially be helpful if you are both working on healing. Some of the ideas you want to share could be triggering for them, and you might have to tread lightly. Some might jump in and give their advice before you share what's on your mind. Finding the right friend for this can be difficult, but it can be very valuable.

Feeling Loved

If your childhood hurts were seen as a car accident, one part of healing is getting pulled from the wreckage; the second part is the healing that takes place once you are free from the mangled mess. This second part is to see that we deserve love and are loved, independent of our experiences and self-image.

Love is built into our makeup. If you were crossing a street and the stranger next to you fell, you would not pause, get compassion, and then look to see how you could help. Compassion is built into who we are; Love is the source of that compassion. If Love is with my being and that same Love is a transcendent entity that crosses culture and time, I am connected to Love no matter how I was treated as a child.

The newborns I cared for during my forty years in practice also taught me that Love lives within. I observed parents' love for their babies, and this love cut across ages, cultures, and socioeconomic backgrounds. Parents' love for newborns is almost palpable, and their babies did nothing to earn it. They don't even smile or show appreciation for the love bestowed upon them. I also took care of babies in neonatal intensive care units. These sick and premature infants not only did nothing to earn their parents' love, but they also were even in the negative column; they had problems. But the love for these babies seemed even more powerful than that for their healthy counterparts. We know this. If someone we cared about was going to give birth to a baby who would need open heart surgery soon after delivery, our love and support would go out to them in powerful ways.

If a parent couldn't care for their baby and the assigned caregiver didn't express love, the love surrounding that baby wouldn't change. Newborns are imbued with Love. We were all babies. Whether our childhood made this experience obvious or not, we are all connected to Love.

The tools of Focused Inner Listening can also help us feel filled with Love, replacing the notion that we are unloved and unlovable.

- While lying in bed, open to Love and feel it.
- While in bed, on walks, during journaling, and when talking with friends, appreciate that you are loved and filled with Love.
- Your caregivers' shortcomings determined how they raised you, and this was not connected in any way to your being deserving of love. Have imaginary conversations with your younger self in bed, while journaling, or on long walks. Tell that

child that you love them and that you will always
be together.

- Review this at odd times during the day.

I saw a physical representation of the power in this work
when I observed an eighth-grade physics class beginning
the study of light. The teacher prepared the room by closing
the lab's blackout shades and all other lights, including all
LEDs. When Mr. Tomlinson turned off the overhead lights,
darkness enveloped the room. I couldn't even see my fingers
moving when I put my hand in front of my face, and this
didn't change with time. There was no low level of light for
my eyes to readjust to. It was completely dark. We sat in
that darkness. He'd asked the students to remain quiet, and
they did so. After what seemed like an extraordinarily long
time, Mr. T quietly lit a candle in the front of the room.
That tiny bit of light was so exhilarating that some students
involuntarily gasped. Letting the slightest amount of light
into our inner darkness is equally dramatic.

Healing Ongoing Trauma

Healing also includes the time between childhood insults
and the present.

Our childhood hurts left many with a wide range of
psychological challenges that included anxiety, depression,
low self-esteem, alcohol and drug abuse, poor relationships,
anger, and poor school effort. These had effects on the course
of our lives, leading to our present conditions. Healing
begins with both forgiving ourselves and objectively taking

stock. We can forgive ourselves for what we did in a way that fits under the legal umbrella known as *the fruit of a poisoned tree.* Evidence obtained illegally is considered the fruit of a poisoned tree and cannot be admitted to trial. The actions stemming from our childhood hurts are the fruits of a poisoned psyche. We were hurting because of what happened; we weren't ourselves, and we can therefore forgive ourselves for what happened.

At the same time, we did what we did, which must also be addressed. We need to assess the damage we caused objectively and the people we hurt so we can develop a plan to fix what we can. We might need to apologize to someone we hurt, undertake specific actions to address what we did, or, seeing that we cannot change some things, commit to acting differently. Making friends with who we are and what we value and seeing the good in ourselves are all important. Work on these using the steps of Focused Inner Listening. Here are some ways to do so:

- Think about your most important values. See how you've kept them through your life.
- Think about your inner gifts—kindness, honesty, sincerity, faithfulness—whichever is true. Dig through your thoughts and experiences. Find what's truly yours.
- I imagine writing who you are on a small scroll, capturing your best self in a sentence or two. What would you write?

Forgiveness

We can't heal without forgiveness. My mom argued with a lifelong friend. My sister and I were adults and remained friendly with our mother's new enemy. She wanted us to take sides; not doing that, in her mind, let her friend off the hook. She couldn't do that; she couldn't forgive her. This view of forgiveness differs from the forgiveness that will be described here. We don't have to oversee the punishment of those we forgive, though we should discuss their actions with the authorities if they did anything illegal or threatened others. Holding onto our anger only keeps us in the past, like a splinter in the paw. With it in place, we cannot go forward.

Forgiveness doesn't even include the other person's awareness. If it did, they would have to appreciate the wrong they did, acknowledge it, and be a part of our forgiveness. In my experience, those who hurt us are often the same person they always were and are unaware of how they hurt us. Even if they know they might not have been perfect, they are often not big enough to admit it to the one they hurt.

We don't need them to admit the wrongs they did to us to forgive. We can forgive them without them even knowing that we've forgiven them, and here are four different ways to do this. One more will be added in a later chapter.

- **Deathbed forgiveness:** This approach to forgiveness is directed toward a person who has hurt you badly. It's imagining that the person who hurt you is on their deathbed. They don't recognize who you are and ask you to close the window and to put an extra blanket on them. In this kind of forgiveness, we can imagine ourselves doing that without taking anything from the past. We simply see a dying person who is cold.

- **Wedding or business gathering forgiveness:** This kind of forgiveness is directed toward those who hurt you, but not as much as in *deathbed forgiveness.* These can also be people who later in life hurt you in business or through a relationship. We imagine we are at a wedding, a family gathering, or a business event, and the person who hurt us is there. This type of forgiveness includes appreciating that nobody at the event wants to be a part of, or even know, that there is any animosity between us. We treat the person as if nothing ever happened. We might even need to talk with them or sit at the same table. Still, we let nothing of the past percolate into the present. Sometimes, this kind of forgiveness is practiced in real-life situations.

- **Diamond forgiveness:** In an episode of the old television show, Superman took a piece of coal, squeezed it with extreme pressure, and turned it into a diamond. This kind of forgiveness is aimed at those who achieved *wedding or business gathering forgiveness* but still blame the other person for the events and the repercussions, such as blaming a parent for our relationship issues or a business partner who stole from us for our various financial difficulties. In this kind of forgiveness, all the carbon dust particles—all that you blame the other person for—are gathered together to form a diamond. You stop blaming them. Things are as they are, and you move forward from that.

- **Going to the source forgiveness:** Few experience this kind of forgiveness. It consists of returning to the place where the greatest insults in our lives occurred and fully letting go of the setting's control over us.

  - Wayne Dyer, the late writer, described such an event at his abusive father's graveside. He tracked down the burial site of the man he hadn't seen since he was three and yelled at him for all the pain he'd caused his mother and himself. He then suddenly felt the misery his father had experienced and how that led to his actions and to his leaving. Dyer felt a profound sadness. He cried, forgave him, and walked from the gravesite feeling like a different man. He wrote his first book after this event, writing in a nearby motel. It became a worldwide bestseller.

  - Edith Eva Eger, a psychologist and Holocaust survivor, described going back to Auschwitz years after her internment and letting go of the hold the horrors of the past held over her. This gave Dr. Eger a profound feeling of freedom and the ability to help others.

◻ A friend moved away from her abusive family when she was eighteen. Years later, after her parents had both died, she returned to her home to get it ready for sale. As she dug through the items left behind, memories flooded her. She cried and felt a catharsis that allowed her to step away feeling whole.

Reflections

- Do you see the value in forgiveness?
- Which kind of forgiveness would be the hardest for you to achieve? The easiest?

Additional Ideas

Develop an avatar to symbolize your freedom, such as a caterpillar becoming a butterfly or a person breaking out of chains. When you need a boost, visualize these images in your mind's eye.

You will likely face flashbacks. For example, seeing children playing in a park could lead to unexpected tears if you had a difficult childhood. This is normal. Allow these episodes to pass. If they occur regularly, restart the work on healing that you have already done.

Self-Love

Self-love is a valued psychological state and could even be considered an aim of inner healing, but it has to be understood to appreciate its value. Self-love is not about falling in love with ourselves. If that were its meaning, self-love would make us obnoxious and self-centered. Instead, self-love is feeling so good about ourselves that we can let go and be present. We could see this during a sensitive moment in a relationship or a decisive spot in a sporting event, where self-love allows us to be present, unaware of ourselves, and without negative thoughts about ourselves getting in the way.

Prescription

The steps of Focused Inner Listening:

- Regularly think about the idea
- Work on healing before falling asleep
- Have a written dialogue to work through these ideas
- Take walks to think and to scream at those who hurt you
- Talk with friends about your insights
- Speak with a counselor if any of this is too difficult for you

The following prescription is for a path to letting go of needless worry.

PRESCRIPTION III
Letting Go of Worry

East Twin Lake in Western Connecticut froze with a large section of thick, black-appearing ice—clear ice without any white mixed into it. Fish and weeds moving in the water below were visible, and the ice made cracking and howling sounds as it stretched and shrank. This smooth, flat surface was ideal for skating, but I couldn't bring myself to do so; I was worried it wouldn't hold. In reality, the surface was thick enough to support a truck. Worries often prevent us from enjoying life, and this section teaches us how to rid ourselves of needless worry.

Korine's parents were going to be traveling for work for two weeks during the summer, and they looked for an affordable activity for her to do while they were away. A friend told them about an outdoor adventure camp, and they thought Korine would like it. She was interested when they told her about it, but she was worried about sleeping in a tent and cooking outdoors, two things she had never done. The camp didn't allow any form of electronic communication or game-playing. She also thought not having her phone sounded impossible, and she didn't know if she'd have the strength and ability for some of the activities, having never rock climbed or gone rafting. The director and one of the counselors came to the house to review the program with the family. Korine liked them, and their responses to her questions allowed her to put her worries and self-doubt aside.

Once at the camp, this inner-city girl liked it from the outset. She slept in a tent, cooked with her campmates, and talked around the fire. She enjoyed activities that were new to her: strenuous mountain hikes, rock climbing, navigating whitewater rapids in a raft, and a two-day solo hike.

Her enthusiasm encouraged others, while her physical ability helped some of her fellow campers overcome obstacles they might not have gotten past on their own. She enjoyed herself so much that, when camp was over, she had a hard time with her former friends, whose worries and concerns seemed trivial. She had also begun to miss the adventures. I saw her that fall for her physical. That's when she told me about the trip.

Had Korine not dropped her concerns about spending nights in a tent and sleeping bag, eating food she wasn't used to, and being unable to communicate with her friends, she would not have enjoyed her trip as much. Had self-doubt gotten in the way, she would not have succeeded in tackling activities she had never faced. Korine has a lot to teach us about worry. We each have our challenges—working to create a nurturing home environment, navigating the tasks in the workplace, and the difficulties in creating a life that works for us—and our attitude means everything. Worry often prevents us from living fully and enjoying life.

This section presents ways to let go of needless worry. We can go to sleep and wake up without worrying and without bouts of worry filling us during the day.

Worry's Different Faces

To understand how we can control worrying, we must first understand its different roles. Some concerns remind us of things needing our attention, like paying taxes on time. These are occasional and fleeting and disappear as soon as we attend to the matter, and they are the only kinds of worry that have value.

Some worries fill our minds when planning an event. A couple might have concerns about all the details of their upcoming wedding as they arrange them. These worries play no role in actually getting the work done, and they can spoil the couple's mood. If these worries persist and spill into the event, it takes the bride and groom out of the moment and prevents them from enjoying the wedding.

Some worries linger, such as concerns for adult children or aging parents. These worries can seep into our interactions with those we worry about and have a negative effect.

Worries always assume a poor outcome and spiral with negativity. If we lose our jobs, we don't become concerned that we'll be overwhelmed by the number of new job offers we'll receive or that we'll earn so much in our new position that our spouse might want to move to a more expensive neighborhood. Instead, worries cloud our minds, take us out of the moment, and prevent us from living fully.

We somehow feel it's our duty to worry about everything, believing that we aren't doing our job if we don't do so, and so we hold on to our worrying. But this is an entirely false idea. We don't need to worry and would be happier if we dropped this habit.

Reflections

- Worry serves no purpose.
- Do you see the negative aspects of worry?
- Are you willing to let go of worrying? If not, why not?

The Presence of Wisdom

Korine's parents thought she would like the outdoor adventure program, and she did. Her experience would likely lead to some positive effects. She might work at the camp the following summer and look for similar activities during the school year. Her new sense of self could take her in fresh directions. Had she not liked the camp, her parents would have looked for a different activity for the following summer, and her life would have taken her down a different path.

Love carries another name: Wisdom, for the heart's love is also wise. We know this in the simplest of ways. If we love a child, enjoy gardening, or care for a pet, we go beyond our ideas and act on their behalf—we act wisely. Similarly, the wisdom within also places us in opportunities to help us grow and expand while preserving our independence and freedom. We don't always see these strings of connection. They are ours to discover. Not only did the idea of the camp come to Korine's parents through outer events, but their wisdom made them think it could be suitable for their daughter.

My life led me to feel that a wise entity was at work through my daily activities. Through this, I realized that if Love is with me in one setting, it has to be present in all my life's circumstances. This reality presents a way to drop worries. I will describe a few times when I knew that something outside of me was at work, and then we'll see how this can be used on our end. While these don't prove anything, they do open a door. I also review them to help you think about parallel situations in your own life.

I was sitting on a park bench, sipping coffee and reading the newspaper one Sunday, when I was working in Manhattan. I was content with my life and had no thoughts of changing anything, when an advertisement on three-inch-wide glossy, beige cardstock fell out of the newspaper and onto my lap. The ad caught my attention, and it described a pre-med program at Columbia University for college graduates who wanted to go to medical school but still needed to take the required math or science courses. As I read the piece, an image of a man in his forties having a heart attack came to mind. He would want a physician to care for his medical problems, and I also imagined he'd have a lot of pressing questions: what does this mean to my life? How do I go forward? What do I tell my family and friends? He'd want to discuss these, and he'd do so with the same physician who was treating his medical condition. At that moment, I saw that a physician's career combines complex intellectual challenges with powerful interpersonal concerns, and I knew that was what I wanted to do. I enrolled in the program and went to medical school after its two-year course of study. Many factors went into sitting on that park bench and embarking on this course of study, and the odds of this all being due to chance went beyond reasonable analysis.

It took me time to appreciate the hand of Wisdom in my becoming a physician, but I also observed Love's involvement in my life directly and immediately. One such event took place on the Pine Ridge Reservation in South Dakota.

When I was in college, I came across *Black Elk Speaks: The Life Story of an Ogalala Sioux Holy Man*, an autobiography that described the life of this Native American and the ways of his people. It offered a glimpse into their close connection to the natural world and the Great Spirit and moved me deeply.

Black Elk spent his youth in the beautiful and varied Lakota lands, which ranged from the Black Hills to the banks of the Mississippi in the 1860s. At nine, a powerful vision came to him at the summit of Mount Harney (now called Black Elk Peak). The vision concerned itself with his people's sacred hoop and the difficulties they would face. The elders felt it was so important that the tribe performed the nine-year-old's vision as if it were a play.

I had the opportunity to work as a pediatrician at Pine Ridge when I was between jobs and waiting for my credentialing to go through before starting a new one. After completing my work at the Pine Ridge clinic, I headed to the Badlands to hike. On the way, I wondered if Black Elk's old cabin was still standing. I asked about it at several places, but no one could tell me where it was. A green road sign announced that I was in Manderson, South Dakota, and my jaw dropped. That was where Black Elk had lived, where he told his life story to John Neihardt, a historian who came to his home to capture it. While they sat on the log cabin's porch, Black Elk's wife and granddaughter made cookies and lemonade for them.

I decided to give finding the cabin one last try before leaving the area and stopped in at an isolated grocery store along the road. I asked the person behind the counter if he knew where Black Elk's old cabin was. "Why do you want to know?" he asked.

I told him that Black Elk's life story meant a lot to me, and I would be honored to see the old place. "Ask that man over there," the grocer said, pointing to a man near the door. "Hurry up and catch him," he scolded when I hadn't moved quickly enough for his taste.

The tall, well-built, bronze-skinned man standing by the door looked at me somewhat coldly when I asked him about the cabin. "Why do you want to know?"

I also told him about Black Elk's life's influence on me. "Follow me down the road. You'll see a house on the right. There'll be a red truck and a blue truck in the driveway. That's my house. Go in and ask for my mother, Esther Black Elk DeSersa. She's Black Elk's granddaughter."

The one-story house stood alone on the flat, dry land, covered by a vast blue sky. Trucks dotted the dirt driveway, and I pulled in. The person I'd been following was no longer in sight. I stood at the door, feeling awkward and unsure about what to do. I finally knocked, and someone asked what I wanted. I told him that I was looking for Esther Black Elk. He shouted, "Someone's looking for you, grandma," when she asked who was there. They opened the door and welcomed me in. After introducing myself and shaking the older woman's hand, we talked on a couch in the living room. I told her about my interest in the book and said that I remembered reading that she and her grandmother baked cookies for Black Elk and his biographer. Now in her eighties, she reflected on those days and told me she'd never read his book. "I couldn't. What happened to my people is too sad for me."

I tried reassuring her, telling her the book was important to me and my generation. When I asked, she offered to sign my copy of the book. I got it from my car, and the first page now includes her inscription. "To Ron: Enjoy and Be Happy—Esther Black Elk DeSersa, Granddaughter of Black Elk."

After a while, she asked her grandchildren to take me to the old cabin, and we said goodbye. The old abandoned wooden cabin stood a distance away. I was alone, so I quietly walked there, thinking about those days and what had happened on the front porch.

I regularly experience the presence of the Divine in many small ways. The other day, for example, I was putting my sweatshirt into the hamper when my hand brushed against something in its pocket—my wallet. I had put it there when I went out to run an errand that morning. I would have thrown it in with the wash if not for this accidental contact with my wallet. I felt goosebumps and was certain that I was receiving assistance.

With time, I had to know if this was true: was Love always with me, and was my life filled with Wisdom? I'd read such ideas in many of the books I liked and heard people say things like, "It's all for the good," and "Things work out for the best." Some speak about synchronicity as if it were a reality. I had to find out if these ideas were correct.

I needed to confirm this concept, and the only method I could think of was to live as if it were true—that I was where I should be and I was not alone. To do this, I realized I could only look at my own life and not consider others' opinions or world events. If my testing was successful, I could expand this concept.

I hypothesized that if the idea were valid, I would be more comfortable, less worried, more present, and fully participate in and enjoy my life. I would be present and able to make better decisions if I were always in the right place. If the idea

I was testing didn't hold, if this thinking didn't match reality, I would feel lost, out of sync, and less capable. I carefully kept my professional life out of this, as my patients could not be a part of this investigation. I planned to test this idea like a scientist working through an experiment. If the ideas didn't hold—if my thinking slipped or I found they didn't improve my quality of life and practical skills—I would drop the experiment and the idea.

I lived as if Love was always with me, that I was always in the right place, and that whatever happened to me had Wisdom behind it. My concept was tested relatively early in this undertaking.

I was traveling to visit my eighty-year-old mom in Florida. She had become a widow, had stopped driving, and resided in a condo within a senior community. After delivering my bag to the curbside check-in at the airport, I drove to the long-term lot and returned to the terminal. When I got to security, I discovered my driver's license was missing. After rifling through my carry-on items and not finding it, I ran back to the curbside check-in counter, where I had to have shown it. It wasn't there either. I panicked. I could get on the plane with other forms of ID, but I couldn't rent a car in Florida. Boarding was twenty minutes away, and I didn't know what to do.

I'd planned several excursions with my mom, and she was excited about them. Traveling made our visits more enjoyable. Without a car, we'd have to stay on the grounds of her small community, and I never liked spending too much time at this senior village. We'd also have to eat all our meals in her small apartment. This would not be a fun vacation for me. Moreover, she would mock me for misplacing my license, making me feel like a child. All the mistakes I ever made would be fresh in her mind.

I then remembered the idea that I was researching: I was in the hands of a loving presence. The Heavenly had to know where my license was; it could only be missing for good reason. I let go of my fears of my mother's likely upset and criticism and looked for a more positive perspective. I was going to my mom's house for a vacation, and we both looked forward to the visit. My mother loved me, and I loved her. I hadn't done anything bad. I had made a mistake. If I didn't get defensive at my mother's giving me a hard time—if I could even give her the space to ridicule me and see me as her child—it would blow over, and our love would surface. We would find ways to have a good time. Another adventure might be waiting, one that required us to be at her place. It was also possible that my planned outings would be too much for her. I didn't know, but I kept myself open, letting the idea take over that Love was in charge.

I was no longer panicked, but I still wanted to find my license and put all my energy into it. I found my license on the top of a pile of papers on the front seat of my truck. I got back to the plane as its doors were about to close. Finding my license wasn't the important point; the mental shift I'd taken and lived with was the key.

This test lasted two years, and the idea that Wisdom is with me stuck. I never stopped the 'experiment.' It's how I now live my life. It allows me to be present, to open my heart to Love, and to stand on solid ground in a wonderfully strengthening way. The reader now stands at a turning point. If Love is with you, then so is Wisdom. You can test it as I have; you can also take my word for it, but that means living as if it's true.

Reflections

- Have you ever felt that something greater was involved in your life's events?
- Have you ever contemplated the notion that if you experienced a higher presence in a single instance of your life, it must be present in all settings?

Using Wisdom to Let Go of Worry

To use this idea to tackle worry, I first had to see that the Divine was involved in the situations that caused me to worry. Most worries fit into the following categories:

- Your health
- Your finances
- Your relationships
- These same areas for people we love
- Concerns about our values, the institutions we care about, and the planet itself

This section will approach the first two. Later chapters will explore the others.

Health

If the heavens were involved in our health and disease, the standard view would see good health as the aim. A change of view, however, appreciates the value of good health but also sees life as a process—it's about growth. Our various states of health and illness go beyond good and bad; they allow us to experience life from multiple perspectives. For example, I've cared for many children with chronic medical problems and physical disabilities. Despite the seemingly unfavorable outcome, an unusually high number of their siblings pursue careers in helping professions. Their emotional connection to the care their loved ones received prompts them to make theirs a life of healing.

Seeing Heaven's hand in health and disease requires a deeper look than our usual cursory one. A mom with two children, a two-month-old and a two-year-old, told me she was leaving her husband during one of their checkups. It's rare for a woman to leave a relationship, especially when her children are so young. Many women stay in unhealthy relationships for much longer than they know they should. I asked why she was leaving him.

She told me that after she delivered her youngest child, some of the fluid that surrounded the baby before birth went to her lungs. This is called an amniotic fluid embolus; it is an extremely rare event and typically fatal. They took her to the intensive care unit, where she intermittently lost consciousness. Visitors told her to be strong and that she would get better. Though barely conscious, she heard these words, reflected on them, and realized that she didn't want to get better. Surprised at her reaction, she looked for the cause of this feeling and saw that her husband was the reason she didn't want to get better. He was often angry, and he got violent. He hadn't hit her, but she was convinced that he would. When she realized that, she knew she had to get out. After telling me this story, she also told me that she did not doubt that this amniotic fluid embolus was a gift to her and her children, allowing her to appreciate the seriousness of her life's circumstances and to act on them.

I went on a week-long summer trip to Nova Scotia several years ago. I was still working, and this was to be a bicycle, hiking, and touring trip. I made lodging reservations around the island's circumference and planned to take day hikes and bike rides. I took a ferry from Portland, Maine, across the Gulf of Maine with my car, but the night before the trip, I had excruciating pain in my right arm. I could barely close my fist. I was otherwise well, and knew I wasn't having a heart attack. I thought the pain was from pinched nerves, a version of what's called carpal tunnel syndrome. Something I'd had before.

The pain was severe when I put pressure on my hand or turned my arm the wrong way, and it prevented me from putting on or carrying a backpack. Hiking and bike riding were out. I was able to type on my laptop without discomfort, and I wondered if I was being told to write instead of riding my bicycle or hiking.

I had a great trip, enjoyed seeing the countryside, and took small excursions, like an afternoon trip on a small boat to follow whales. I also wrote a lot. I developed a hypothesis: if the pain was telling me that I should spend the time working on this book and was not due to a significant medical problem, my arm would be fine once the trip was over. That's exactly what happened. I returned to Portland, stayed the night there, and the pain was completely gone.

Money

Our finances affect all aspects of our lives, providing us with opportunities to set and test our values and decide how we want to live. A personal experience highlighted this for me. After deciding to pursue the pre-med program at Columbia, I met with my parents to inform them and ask for funding. I could only undertake the program with their financial support. My parents didn't have much money, and I reassured them that I would be perfectly happy staying at my current job if they couldn't afford it. Without hesitation, they said they would support me.

My dad died just before I was accepted into medical school, and he never knew I made it. I wore a tie every day to work to honor my dad, thinking he would expect a physician to wear a tie. Years after his death, my mother told me that he never imagined that I would get into medical school; I had been a lackluster student who never took schoolwork seriously. He didn't know why this would suddenly change. Despite this, he gave me his money so I could pursue my dreams. His support for me would not have meant as much had he been wealthy. His actions affected how I am with money with my children and how I approach money in general.

Our financial status affects where we live, work, and who we meet. I went to Queens College, a commuter school at City University of New York, where tuition was $34 per semester. I went there because of the price. Sheldon Stoff, a teacher at Queens College, saw something deeper in me, woke me up, and changed my life. I would not have met him if our family had more money because I would have likely gone to another school.

It became clear that my finances allowed me to set and test my beliefs, meet people, and develop my skills and interests. I still needed a few more steps to implement my ideas about letting go of worry.

Trusting Life

If we knew the future, we wouldn't worry. We might have complex challenges to face, but there would be nothing to worry about. Worries arise because we don't know the future. Therefore, I realized that if I could be okay with the worst outcome to my problems—not the most extreme but the most likely ones—I wouldn't have to worry. I then applied this idea to both my health and finances. Health

There are three distinct categories of health-related issues:

1. Problems that will be entirely resolved

    - Some medical problems will be fully resolved. It might take time and treatment, but I will be the same once they are over. I don't need to worry about these illnesses; instead, I can ponder their possible meaning.

2. Problems that will leave me changed

   - It's hard not to worry when a problem is in flux, but once our new state of health becomes clear, we can consider how we wish to manage it—how we can learn from it, move forward, and still be ourselves. Worry plays no role here.

3. Problems that bring me closer to death

   - When problems arise that bring our deaths close, we can consider how we want to live and whether any of our relationships need attention. Doing this would mean a lot for us and the people involved.

Money

If I could be okay with the reasonably worst way things could turn out, I wouldn't have to worry about my financial situation. Assume, for example, that I lose my job. Considering the worst possible outcomes, I might see that I'd need to move. If I can be okay with that and know that my family and I will adjust, I can drop my worries, be present, and make the best decisions for the future. I needed to add one last piece to put an approach to decreasing worry into action.

Grouping Worries

Some events are out of my control, such as losing my job due to downsizing. If wisdom is built into my life, when something occurs that's out of my control, it has to be in greater hands.

Here is an example of a time when events that seemed terrible in the moment became one of the biggest blessings in my life and the lives of others:

I was about to enter a restaurant on a sunny winter afternoon. Melting New England snow dripped from the roof, leaving an unseen patch of ice under the partially shoveled walkway. My feet went out when they hit that glossy surface, and I fell. My arms immediately went out, stopping my fall and shielding my face from damage. Only my eyeglasses and the tip of my nose were scraped. I'd just missed a severe head injury.

My left wrist wasn't as fortunate. While it broke the fall, the lower end of the big bone in the wrist shattered. The surgeon put all the pieces back together with a plate, and I was out of work for six weeks. A few days after the accident, I learned that a college friend had been diagnosed with end-stage pancreatic cancer. Her ex-husband, who was a friend of mine, told me about her illness. He also told me that he had shared some of my early writings with her and that she found them very interesting. I was home with nothing to do but heal and had speech-to-text software on my computer. I dictated long letters to Ruth and reviewed some of my thoughts about spirituality. We had long, written discussions over the next several weeks.

When my doctor was less concerned that I would bump into someone and reinjure my wrist, she allowed me to leave the house. I went to visit Ruth in the D.C. area.

In college, Ruth had lovely blonde hair and a beautiful smile. She was now gaunt, had thinning gray hair, and was in so much pain that sometimes, she only found comfort by lying flat on the floor. She told me how close she was with her sons, who were both married adults, how proud she was of them, and that she could die because she knew they would be okay.

A month later, she was in hospice care, and I went to visit. She was sedated and not conscious during the time I was there, but a friend who is a palliative care nurse reassured me that she would still be aware. She was lying on her back with crisp white sheets covering all but her neck and face. As I looked at her, I thought of a rock climber dangling over a cliff, holding onto life with her fingers gripping as tightly as possible. I felt she was hanging on because she didn't want to leave her children alone.

We were the only ones in the room. I told her my thoughts and reassured her that she could let go. I reminded her that her kids were okay and knew that she loved them. As I told her she could let go, I began to chant, saying words that just came to me:

> *You live in peace; you breathe out peace. You live in love; you breathe out love.*
> *You come from love; you are filled with love. You are bathed in peace; you radiate peace.*

Her breathing joined the rhythm of my words. When her nurse came in to straighten a few things, I noticed that we had been in a trance-like state. I left while the nurse tidied up. One of her sons and her best friend were in the hallway just outside her door. They'd heard my conversation with Ruth. When the nurse left the room, they asked me to return and continue to talk to her. I did so, and the spaces between Ruth's breaths lengthened. I knew she was letting go. I had her son and friend come in, and we stood holding her hands, telling her that we loved her, and then she stopped breathing.

When I broke my wrist because I slipped on the ice, as strange as it may seem, as soon as I hit the ground, I could see that this event was out of my control. With this, I knew I was not alone, and this appreciation took away worry and upset, allowing me to heal without fear, anger, or regret. My time with Ruth could not have happened without my shattered wrist.

Some worries develop because of my mistakes, such as spilling a drink on my laptop. Accidents only occur when I'm not fully paying attention. Had I been mentally present, the accident would not have happened. If I'm not fully present, the Heavenly has to be there, filling in. This frees me from beating myself up when accidents happen, as they will. I am still responsible for what happened and can learn from it, but I can also be kind to myself. I can also free myself from giving someone else a hard time when they accidentally do something that causes a problem.

My shortcomings also create events that cause worry. I have strengths and weaknesses; I can't be good at everything. The Wisdom that gives me strength also gives me my weaknesses. The unconditional love surrounding us includes our shortcomings. When my shortcomings put me in difficult situations, as they inevitably do, I can remember that Love designed them. They will likely cause problems, but I can lean on a deeper reality and not worry.

I was on my way to an important meeting at work, and I left the house late, and then I hit a traffic jam. I knew I would be late, and I worried about the consequences. I could finally let go of them. I was not alone. I have a tendency to be late, which goes back as far as I can remember. I've tried numerous ways to break this habit, and I've been getting a lot better, but it still rears its head. I'm sure this makes no sense to readers who are always on time. I don't just brush it off and ignore it. I take full responsibility for it. But I know that Wisdom is with me. My shortcomings help me build compassion and forgiveness toward others, for we all have shortcomings.

We now have all the tools we need to let go of our worries. Let's review:

- Love lives within.
- We are always in the right place, and we are never alone.
- We can remember that the hand of Wisdom is with us, and we can use this to drive away fear.
- Whenever our health or finances cause us to worry, we can remember that we are in the hands of Love.
- Sometimes, I am confused and don't know what to do. When I let go of worrying, do what makes

sense, and later see how well what I thought was impossible worked out, my confidence builds, and I can use this when I face hard times.

Reflections

- Could Wisdom be involved in your state of health?
- Could Wisdom be involved in your finances?
- Does it make sense that Wisdom works through our lives?

Putting It All Together

To use these ideas, you first have to make them your own. Focused Inner Listening (see last chapter) helps with this. Think about these ideas at odd moments, before sleep, or when awake at night. Take walks, keep a journal, and talk to friends about these ideas. This work is akin to packing for a trip. If we pack well—once we own these ideas—we can enjoy our journey and be fully present. Living with only occasional, brief worries is a wonderful change.

A Word About Faith

The ideas presented here might seem to rest on faith, and some readers might feel uncomfortable with that. But it's a kind of faith we use daily; it's more like working on a hypothesis. If I hire someone to work in my office, for example, I do so based on references and an interview. Then, I hire the person with faith that my decision will work out.

The ideas presented here carry that same kind of faith. If they make sense to you, carry them out and see if they hold. If they don't serve you well, drop them, just as you would fire the person you hired if they didn't work out. Try them out for a while and then decide.

Prescription

- Worrying does not solve problems.
- If you stopped worrying, nothing would change except how much you worry.

Ways to work through self-doubt, guilt, feelings, and emotions are the next prescription.

PRESCRIPTION IV

Untangling Self-Doubt, Guilt, Feelings, and Emotions

Babies aged four to six months possess the most delightful smiles of childhood. Their whole being laughs when they laugh, and we laugh with them. These moments of presence slowly recede in favor of necessary developmental factors. However, the capacity for this state of innocent delight still resides within. We could call it up and experience such presence and delight, but self-doubt, guilt, and difficult emotions often get in the way. This section reviews how to overcome these barriers.

I was driving through pea-soup fog, and the visibility provided by my car's headlights kept me on the road and out of danger. I started on the coast of Northern California and went inland toward Mount Shasta. At one point, the fog was suddenly gone, with bright sunshine and clear skies ahead of me. The change was so dramatic that I pulled over and got out of my car to look back. I saw a high wall of solid-appearing fog stretched across the horizon behind me.

Likewise, we can leave the dark clouds of self-doubt, guilt, and the swirls of our feelings and emotions to see ahead, bathed in light, whole and intact.

Self-Doubt

Self-doubt eats at how we feel about ourselves. We covered one aspect of self-doubt in the last chapter when we reviewed our shortcomings. Here, we'll look at the term self-doubt from another angle and begin with its meaning. It's not about doubting our existence; we exist. It's questioning our value and whether we are good enough. Here, we must ask who is judging, what is being considered, and what standards are being used.

Shawna's mother brought her in for her nine-month well visit. She also brought Shawna's siblings—three-year-old Max and five-year-old Nevaeh. When I entered the room, Shawna's mom was singing to her, and Max and Nevaeh were quietly playing together. The mood was so sweet. I greeted everyone. Max and Nevaeh returned to their game while I chatted with their mom and examined Shawna. At one point, Nevaeh and Max had a question for their mom. She focused on them, addressed them with warmth and patience, and then redirected them back to their play.

I told her how impressed I was with her and pointed out how sweet her children were and how wonderful she was with them. She shrugged off my compliments as if she didn't believe me, and this reminded me of something I had noticed in other instances: wonderful parents often don't appreciate their parenting skills. I wondered why and eventually concluded that their self-doubt grew from a false idea of being a good parent. Since I wanted this mom to appreciate the value of her hard work, I reviewed what I'd learned about being a good parent, ideas I'd developed through my personal and professional observations.

"Your love is like sunshine to your children; it is the air they breathe, and it fills them. That's all they need. We don't have to be perfect as parents. They can see and work past our shortcomings." I shared some of my background to emphasize my point.

I loved my mother and knew she loved me, but she was far from a good parent. We didn't celebrate birthdays in our house, for example. We didn't have cakes, candles, presents, parties, or special meals. My parents started giving me presents when I was eleven, but they did so without singing "Happy Birthday" and gave me my present unceremoniously. I was given a silver dollar for each year of my life. These weren't wrapped but came with a little Happy Birthday card. This 'card' was actually a torn piece of scrap paper with the words "Happy Birthday" scrawled on it.

I hadn't attended the birthday celebrations other children must have had, so a lack of a party never bothered me. I was also unphased because I knew they loved me. I could work around their actions. I was so untouched by how they handled birthdays that I actually felt sorry for my mother when I was twelve. I was reading my card, and she was by my side. I realized she knew nothing of the joy inherent in giving, and I felt she'd closed herself off to something that could have enhanced her life experience.

We didn't have dinner together, either. My father came home from work at 6:30 p.m. every night and handed me his newspaper. I read the sports section, and he went into our tiny kitchen to have dinner with my mom, where they sat at a table that only fit two. I took my dinner to my bedroom, put it on a folding metal tray, and ate while I watched the TV news. Our dining room table could have easily fit the four of us, and I don't know why we didn't eat together. This didn't bother me either. I liked watching the news, and I, again, had no comparisons. I'd never eaten dinner at anyone else's house; I didn't know that other families sat and talked together during dinner.

Besides relating these stories, I also told this mom that some think they aren't good parents because of a mental image they hold: a good parent is one who never gets frustrated, is always patient, and never tires. She nodded in agreement, saying that was how she measured herself. I told her that this image completely misses the point. "It's not about being perfect," I said. "None of us are. It's about loving our children."

She then said, "Thank you, Dr. Schneebaum. That's just what I needed to hear today." Her shoulders dropped, and she looked so relieved.

This story exemplifies what occurs when an intellectual concept measures a heart-based activity. Had she looked at her parenting with her heart, she would have appreciated how nicely her children played together and how well they listened. The childlike sweetness of their mood made her excellent work clear. We fall short, and self-doubt arises whenever the intellect's critical analysis assesses the loving heart's effort. The heart and the mind speak different languages. This sense of falling short can occur in any sphere of life. The opposite can occur, as well.

Ramon came in for his sixteen-year-old physical. He had never applied himself in school, and I gave him a pep-talk about doing schoolwork, approaching the topic from several angles. I told him that class would be less painful if he did the work, reminding him that he'd be there anyway and could participate in the conversations instead of trying to hide from his teachers, hoping they wouldn't call on him. I also told him that doing schoolwork would help him live a happier life, and not merely because he'd get a better job. Doing schoolwork enables you to develop an underused muscle: your ability to think.

To enjoy life, we sometimes have to think through life's challenges, and this takes work. I know many adults who get tired thinking through a problem and can't do it. Thinking through school problems helps develop mental strength. I told him that if he were a professional athlete and were offered a trade that he could choose to take or not, he'd have to sort out the pros and cons: the various teammates and coaches, the cities, which move would be better for his family, and which made more sense monetarily. Such decisions are like solving an algebra equation with factors on each side.

I saw Ramon several months later. He told me he'd been working hard in school and getting good grades in all his classes except for English, which he was failing. I asked why, and he told me it was because of his teacher. The class was asked to write a paper; it was the first he ever wrote. He worked hard, but the teacher returned it, almost without reading it, and told him it wasn't good enough; he had to do it again. He redid the paper, though motivating himself this second time was harder, and the same thing happened when he handed it in: the teacher told him it wasn't good enough and that he should redo it. He again felt that she'd hardly looked at it, and he thought she didn't like him or was a racist. He'd had it, and he stopped working in her class.

Assuming she was only criticizing his writing, he took her objective criticism personally, as if it were an attack on him. When we take objective criticisms personally, we think we aren't good at the activity, blame someone else for our difficulties, and sometimes shut down.

Reflections

- Are you overly critical of yourself?
- Do you take the opinions of others too seriously?
- Do you take some criticism too personally?

Feeling Guilty

Guilt also affects our feelings about ourselves, and this term also raises questions. The word guilty implies that we've been put on trial and found at fault, but when did this happen? Who tried us? Who was the judge? What standard was used?

We feel guilty when we break the wishes of a *higher authority*. This eats at us, and we think we are bad. The authority who judges us is often our parents, another respected adult, or our religious/ spiritual traditions. When we don't obey their decree, we feel guilty. Sometimes, this is quite dramatic.

A friend of mine married outside of his religion, which ended his relationship with his father, who said the Prayer for the Dead for him. My friend felt terrible. Another friend felt guilty for disobeying her mother's wishes, though her mother never voiced these wishes; she assumed her daughter would know what she wanted. Some adult authorities become upset when we don't take up the careers they prefer, don't dress according to their views, don't love the right people, or don't raise our children the way they think we should. Their views can be so powerful that some don't break them, or they feel bad about themselves when they do. We feel guilty, but we don't need this. We can be fully ourselves and guilt-free.

Getting there is simple—but it's not easy. It matches an aspect of healing childhood hurts reviewed in the last chapter. Our parents' concerns are not ours. If they can't see us because they are so committed to their ideas, if they can't appreciate us as we are and enjoy seeing us find our way, we can't help them. If our choices upset them, it is not our problem. Letting guilt get to us and not living our own lives because of their views makes no sense. We can be ourselves, ignore their worries, and free ourselves from fault.

Occasionally, we can confront this directly. I once had such an opportunity. My mom was a schoolteacher in the New York City public school system and greatly valued her job security, medical insurance, and pension. She'd worked hard and was the only one in her family who had gone to college. I was a schoolteacher after my college graduation and earned a master's degree. After a few years, I decided to leave teaching. I had been in school since I was five years old, and I needed time to think about what I wanted to do and ponder what I valued. If I was going back to teaching, I had to understand the 'whys' of teaching as well as the 'hows.' My mom was devastated by this decision because I was throwing away everything she'd worked so hard to achieve. I sat with her and told her that I had to make my own choices with my life. I was young and had a lot to learn. She could either support me or give me a hard time, and I added that I would love to have her support. She rose to the occasion and did exactly that; she never gave me a hard time about leaving teaching, even with my going off to work in a logging camp in the Alaskan wilderness after my stint as a teacher. I was amazed she could drop her concerns; it was so helpful. Sometimes, overcoming guilt takes a lot of work, but we have no choice: it's our life.

Religious/spiritual practice can also overpower us with guilt by telling us what to do to be in God's good graces, feel Divine Energy, or stay on the good path. This can include how often we should attend religious services or how long we should pray or meditate. The rules often tell us what to wear, who to love, and how to live our lives. We are told that when we break God's commandments or don't pray, meditate, or celebrate holidays, we suffer, and not following these rules and precepts clouds how we feel about ourselves. I know many who think they aren't as good as they should be because their actions cause them to sacrifice their higher potential. This is false. We can listen to ourselves and follow what directly works for us.

This might be a challenging move for some, but it's based on the idea that God, Christ, or Divine Energy live within each of us. This puts a very different spin on the question of guilt. We can open to this Inner Light, but only if we feel it nourishes us. The Light Within is always there. It loves us and appreciates our struggles. We are never alone.

This does not suggest that one shouldn't enjoy their religious or meditative practices. If they bring feelings of connectedness and value, enjoy them. If they don't, then don't let feelings of guilt make you think you're loved any less or judged for being true to yourself. The Heavenly enjoys our struggles and quietly roots for us.

Reflections

- Is guilt a significant factor in your decision-making?
- Do your feelings of guilt spring from your religion or your elders?
- Can you see how to let go of feeling guilty?
- Are you willing to let it go? If not, why not?

Feelings and Emotions

Feelings, in this discussion, are the experiences that stem from our physical nature, such as feeling thirsty, tired, pleased, or afraid. The term also refers to our responses to these signals, such as feeling good after eating and the relief felt when pulled from danger. Person-to-person variability exists within these basic feelings. Some enjoy the mouth-burn of spicy foods and the feeling of freefall on a roller coaster or while skydiving, and others don't.

Thinking can override our basic physical feelings, and that's one of the things that makes us human. If we were tired and an ill loved one needed us, our tiredness would melt away in service to the other, and some people, like rescue workers, prioritize their safety but put that aside for the benefit of others. Dogs can't similarly decide to stop chasing squirrels and have lunch with them instead, and lions cannot choose to eat a more plant-based diet.

Emotions

The Parkers were driving to the hospital to have their first baby when Sheila said, "Pull over and call 911. I can't hold back. This baby is coming."

Cliff did that, put the phone on speaker mode, and they followed the instructions for delivering their baby. They were also told that an ambulance was sent and would be arriving soon.

They remained calm and followed the directions, and just as Jessica's dad was putting a blanket around her, the ambulance arrived. The EMTs took her momentarily, examined her, cared for the cord, and then returned Jessica to her parents. The emotions they'd held back burst once their baby was safely in their arms; they cried and hugged each other while staring at their adorable newborn.

Emotions arise when we engage with the world and feel accepted, rejected, or not in control.

- A line formed at the ice cream truck. Four-year-old Amber watched and told her dad that she wanted ice cream. He said she couldn't have any, as they were eating soon. Her pleading didn't change his mind, so she yelled, kicked, and screamed, turning her rejection into a full-blown tantrum.
- I was playing a baseball card game at my friend Steven's house. The winner kept the other players' cards. I was ten years old and lost all of my cards to him. I responded by sitting on the couch with a sad face. His mother saw me and asked what had happened. I told her, and she made him return my cards.
- Manny's mom brought him to my office because she was concerned about her 16-year-old son's frequent anger outbursts. He and I talked about this, and we met for several sessions. It eventually became clear that his underlying upset was the loss of his father; he'd left the family when Manny was three. Manny had no dad, and he didn't like seeing his mom struggle. The upset within him made him feel on edge.

There is nothing inherently wrong with our commonly termed 'negative emotions.' These mostly unconscious responses arise when life doesn't work the way we want it to, causing the upset we feel in our bodies that surfaces in our emotions and actions. The upset Amber felt in her rejection resulted in the temper tantrum she used to change her father's mind. Pouting was a strategy I'd developed to get what I wanted, and Manny's upset led to generalized anger. While there's nothing 'wrong' with these emotions and the responses generated from them, they don't get us where we want to go.

If Amber continued to have temper tantrums as an adult, she might get the things she wants, but happiness wouldn't be one of them. I was an adult when I discovered that sulking was not an efficient way to handle loss and that a more mature and practical approach was needed. Manny could potentially see that his anger wouldn't bring his father back. If he didn't act on that, his father's actions would etch themselves into his thinking and prevent him from being himself.

Raw emotions are like the winds that could toss a sailboat around. We can steer the ship and enjoy a day on the water by working the sails and using a centerboard, a fin-like structure that goes into the water lengthwise along the middle of the boat. These keep us upright and allow us to use the wind to move us in our desired direction. The sails and centerboard are our thinking with our hearts and minds. As in the following story, we can align our emotions with who we are and how we wish to be.

A childhood friend was in Boston on a business trip, and she called to invite me to dinner. I decided to go because of our long history, but I felt dread during this conversation. Later, I sat by myself, closed my eyes, and explored this feeling. I saw that her voice reignited memories of her constant criticism. I felt under attack when I was with her. I looked at our past more closely and noticed something unexpected: we always had good times together. In this instant, I saw that she didn't dislike me, but she was very critical, which hurt me and made me feel that I was under attack. I then noticed that this was just her style: she asked penetrating questions with a dry tone. I'd interpreted this as being critical, and I could now see that she'd always cared about me, was interested in who I was, and spoke the same way to others. With this in mind, I realized I could let go of my false interpretation of how she talked to me, and I pictured the two of us together enjoying each other's company. I held this image for a while. That night, we had one of our most excellent times together. It was great to reconnect, and we've been closer since then.

The approach I used can help you evaluate your emotional responses and align them with who you are in a step-by-step process:

- **Step 1: Notice what you are feeling**. I felt uncomfortable when I spoke to my friend. This process uses our sense of self and well-being as described in the first chapter.

- **Step 2: Notice the cause of your feelings.** The conversation with my childhood friend caused the experience.

- **Step 3: Become curious about your experience.** How did this conversation create a feeling of discomfort? I felt under attack when she asked me questions, which reminded me of my earlier experiences with her.

- **Step 4: Look at the truth of your experience.** Did my feelings, my sense of being attacked, match reality? I combed through past encounters and saw that we actually had good times together. What I interpreted as her criticism was her very matter-of-fact way of asking questions. She wanted to know how I was and what I thought. There didn't seem to be warmth in her questioning, but it wasn't personal; that was just her style. I saw this in how she related to others I knew. She wasn't being negative; she liked me and was interested in how I was.

- **Step 5: Make a plan.** I could now hear her questions without seeing them as her being critical. My job wasn't to fix her; she didn't ask me to do that. She asked me to join her for dinner and rekindle a friendship. I could do that.

- **Step 6: Imagine this new reality:** I pictured us enjoying each other's company. We had one of the best times that evening, and my new view recharged our relationship.

A few notes:

The first two steps can be worked on as they occur, such as noticing how you feel as the feeling arises, and its source could also be noted immediately. The other work might need to be thought about at a separate time: at odd moments during the day, when lying down before sleep, during meditative/prayer time, during walks set aside for the purpose, or while journaling, just as described when reviewing Focused Inner Listening in Chapter 2. This work can also be done with a friend or a mental health professional if it is too much to tackle alone.

The same process can be used when we feel rejected, whether personal or a rejection of our ideas. While near the nurses' station at my office, I overheard a nurse and one of the medical assistants talking about an office gathering they'd gone to the night before. My stomach dropped, and I felt terrible. I then went through the same steps to see why I felt this pit in my stomach.

I noted what I was feeling. I felt hurt.

I noticed the cause. I'd heard someone talk about a party I wasn't invited to.

I became curious about the feeling. I felt rejected.

I looked at the truth of the experience. I examined my not being invited to the party and saw several possibilities:

1. I didn't receive an invitation because this wasn't my group of friends. I was close with the people in my office, but that didn't necessarily mean we had an out-of-office friendship. Others did have that closeness.
2. I might need to examine how I am seen in the office and learn to fit in better.

I was sure the first of these was true. I would have declined the invitation if asked. I also remembered a time in graduate school when I decided that I would rather not have a date on a Saturday night than go out with someone I didn't especially want to see. Though I'd made that decision, I felt miserable being home alone when that Saturday night arrived. The feeling I was currently experiencing seemed to parallel that. I then appreciated that I was okay with not being invited; it was not personal.

I made a plan. I could let go of feeling rejected and enjoy the office staff liking each other enough to go out and have a good time together. That would only improve the mood in the office.

Ideas sometimes get rejected. During my career, I noticed how many colleagues and co-workers experienced burnout and saw how workplace wellness could be furthered. I was nearing retirement and formed my ideas into a proposal that included a new Department of Wellness, something that existed in other major medical institutions, and I would head it. I invested significant time and energy into this project, and my proposal was rejected. The process just described helped with this.

I noted the rejection. It happened, and there was no doubt about it.

I examined the cause. My ideas were delivered to the proper panel for my proposal's acceptance or rejection. This group had the needed power to decide.

I became curious about the rejection. I had to think about the reasons for the rejection.

- My ideas might not have been presented clearly. My poor description, not my ideas, might actually have been rejected.
- My proposal required a dramatic reorganization, which might have been too much for this large organization to adopt quickly.
- My lack of credentials for this undertaking—as a primary care pediatrician with no management background — could have led to its rejection.
- Someone might have rejected my ideas because they didn't think I was the right person for the job or didn't like me for whatever reason.

I then made a plan. The actual reason for my rejection didn't matter; my proposal was rejected, and I had to decide how to proceed.

If I had presented a similar proposal to my department earlier in my career, I would have had to determine whether I wanted to work where my ideas didn't align with how my department approached things; I could use this as a reason to leave, or I could also be okay with my thoughts not being accepted. My real job was to be with my patients, which wasn't infringed upon. Once I decided, I could move on and let it go.

Sometimes, we face frustration.

Some drivers bang on their horns when they get cut off in parking lots, leaving the person who blew their horn upset for blocks afterward, cursing and mumbling as they drive away and upsetting everyone else in the car. If such a driver went through the same steps, they would notice that they were upset: someone cut them off and could have hurt them. If they became curious about it, they could appreciate that there are a lot of bad drivers. They could also remember times when they accidentally cut someone off.

They hit the horn to awaken the other driver and say, "You idiot.

How could you have done that? You almost crashed into me."

This was done with the hope that the other driver would notice, get out of their car, apologize, and promise never to drive that way again. That doesn't happen, though. The action only causes upset. A new plan could be developed: the formerly angry driver could realize the other person had made a mistake and feel glad they hadn't gotten into an accident. That would be it. They would be happier, and so would everyone else in the car.

Our frustration can be our teacher.

A solo mom in my practice found it challenging to leave the house on time. Five-year-old Jonathan often dawdled. She'd yell at him as her frustration increased, but that almost always caused him to slow down even more. She'd assumed he was aware of time, knew his mom had to leave, and she expected him to get going with his mom's prompt. But children aren't miniature adults who are self-reflective in the way she imagined. Instead, he felt her mood and crumbled.

She also told me that when she got up early, got herself ready, and then woke him up, there was never a problem. She was with him as he got ready, and they got out on time. Yelling or getting angry with another when we are frustrated never helps. We yell at the people we are closest to because we think they see the world the way we do. When they don't act as we would, we yell, thinking that will wake them up. But this never works. If we discover that we are yellers, we must see that those we yell at don't understand what we want. We need to step back, rethink, and take a fresh approach.

When outer events don't go our way, we can also remember that wisdom and love work through our lives. I had a busy solo practice attached to our house, and it was on eight acres of land in a Boston suburb. We had horses, beautiful flower gardens, a small playground near the office, and the most outstanding nurse, receptionist, and support staff.

Some families picnicked before their visits. I felt that this supportive space could begin the healing process.

When I first began in medicine, the diagnosis of attention deficit hyperactivity disorder (ADHD), or ADD, as it was initially termed, was infrequent. With time, I increasingly saw children with the diagnosis, and I developed expertise in the area. The kids I was treating opened my eyes at some point, and I appreciated a different view of the problem.

I asked parents of children diagnosed with ADHD who had no other behavioral problems to tell me about the most vital qualities in these children, the ones that would stand the test of time. Almost all spoke of kids who were caring, kind, and creative. We were missing something, for those qualities are not uniformly present in children with other medical issues.

I noticed that some people are more heart based, and others are more intellectual by nature. Heart based people have a hard time doing work that doesn't fill them with meaning, while those who are more intellectual complete assigned tasks matter-of-factly. School becomes difficult for those with ADHD, and so do many of the demands of life. The same students, though, can be wonderfully creative and hard-working when interested in a task. I sometimes call it *Enthusiasm and Love of Life Disorder.*

I was so struck by what I learned that I decided to leave my practice to change medicine's perspective and approach to ADHD. I opened a counseling practice, worked on a book, and envisioned a retreat area where I could work with families and teachers.

I created a nonprofit organization for the retreat center and wrote mailers asking for support from potential contributors. I put the stack of these mailers on the kitchen counter and had breakfast before going to the post office. I was watching TV when the second of the Twin Towers went down; the other had already been hit. It was the morning of 9/11. I appreciated that this was not the right time to ask for money to fund a new approach to ADHD. The country's interest was elsewhere.

I finished my book, was very happy with it, and had it on editors' desks at four major publishing companies. One showed interest, but the marketing department at that company insisted on having a tangible alternative to medication. In the end, all rejected it. Very few people attended my counseling practice. I had no credentials, and few referred children to me.

I had not only taken a year off; I left the practice and sold the house. It was time to earn a living again. I joined a pediatrician who told me he wasn't interested in my nontraditional approach and just wanted me to be a regular pediatrician. I inwardly knew I should join him, but I had to figure out how to incorporate what I had learned into my work.

The diagnosis of ADHD caused many wonderful children to be seen in a negative light, and many saw themselves negatively. I decided to focus on building bonds between parents and their children and helping young people recognize the good in themselves. I treated the children with ADHD in the traditional manner and also explained my fresh view.

I now see that I am much better off with how things went. Instead of trying to create a soapbox to tell everyone they were wrong and that I was right, I found a way to put my energy into supporting the relationship between parents and their children. This is a better fit for me.

We can review our values and aims and know that Wisdom is with us when we don't get our way.

Prescription

- Instead of doubting ourselves, we can *be* ourselves.
- We can trust our own insights and decisions and step away from the judgments of others.
- Emotions arise when we interact with the world and feel accepted, rejected, or frustrated.
- Our 'negative' emotions serve us if we use them as a signal that we should pause and reflect.

The next prescription will present ways to develop meaningful and rewarding relationships.

PRESCRIPTION V

Developing Rewarding Relationships

Olympic divers standing on the edge of high boards free their minds from all they've learned. Nothing but the present exists as they push through the dive's twists, turns, and flips. Quality relationships also require our full presence as we step into them with all our being. This section teaches how we can do this and have increasingly meaningful relationships.

A group of students in the fifth-grade class I taught reminded me of my friends when I was that age. Communicating with them was easy. A shy, somewhat socially awkward boy who didn't have a lot of self-confidence taught me something else: my job was to help him feel comfortable in the class, and I was not a good teacher until I was able to do so. This chapter is about learning to connect with others. We all get along easily and well with some people, but if we can make connections where they don't come that easily, we will find that we've tapped into a wellspring of richness and meaning that goes beyond our imagination. This section reviews ways to get past the barriers and stumbling blocks that stand in the way of such connections. We'll start with our incidental interactions and work toward our closest ones.

Relationships We Didn't Choose

People who work in restaurants, stores, and gas stations and those who deliver goods to us serve our needs. That's their job. These are often entry-level positions with low-level pay, and these employees frequently work in unfavorable conditions. Their demanding customers, co-workers, and bosses make their tasks even more challenging.

Those who serve us in the offices of the medical professionals we frequent often receive patient complaints about issues over which they have no control, are pressured to do their jobs well, and might have difficult and unreasonably demanding bosses. Our relationships with such people should begin by feeling grateful for their efforts on our behalf, a factor that positions us to think about how we can lighten their burden.

"Could I have two ten-dollar bills for a twenty, please?" I asked the woman behind the register at the gas station.

It was 11:00 in the evening. I had nothing on my mind, and while she made change, I asked, "How's it going?" sensing that she might have had a tough night.

"Not good," she said. "It's been crazy. I almost quit. One guy started cursing at me because we didn't have the brand of mustard he wanted. I've got Crohn's disease, and it's been acting up. (I was shocked that she readily revealed her medical condition to a stranger.) Another guy cursed at me because he was in a hurry and the pump was too slow."

"It's nuts out there. Don't let them get you," I said as I thanked her for the change.

After our brief exchange, she stood taller and seemed more relaxed. Being heard and appreciated made a difference in her mood. I spent no extra time, and our interaction left her feeling better. Helping someone else also made me feel good.

Neighbors

We don't choose our neighbors, but we do choose how we interact with them. Friendliness enhances our environment. We might also wish for a close enough connection to ask for a favor, like asking them to bring in a package if we are away or to check that we turned our oven off. At its most basic, being a good neighbor is a simple "Hello. How are you?"

Our neighbors might be difficult people, but as long as their actions don't threaten our safety or prevent us from being comfortable in our homes, we can work to figure out how to create a friendly relationship. No one who is grumpy is content. There is no set rule on how to proceed. Sometimes, commiserating helps, and listening to their concerns might make a difference; for others, it's a kind act. Our kindness can also be of value to our neighbors in ways we can't imagine.

A friend had a casual 'hello' relationship with her elderly neighbor, who was frail and lived alone. She always asked how he was and ended their conversations by saying, "So nice to see you. Be well."

They spoke for longer than usual one day, and this neighbor shared that my friend's inquiry into his well-being and her wishing him well gave him a good feeling that lasted throughout his entire day.

Relationships at Work

Some office interactions involve staff members who aren't in our work pool, and we can work to keep these relationships friendly.

Our other office relationships are with those we work with directly. The quality of work takes precedence, with our camaraderie feeding off our work. Hospital-based code teams epitomize this. They respond when a patient's heart or breathing stops, with each member playing a role developed by the American Heart Association at a code: one oversees the airway, one takes the heart, one manages fluids, and others round out what's needed to maximize recovery. They practice together, work together, and review what they did when the code is over. The intensity of their work and the quality of their performance build bonds. They can have very different lifestyles and interests and not be close outside of work, but their effort brings them together in the office.

That same intensity isn't as obvious in other work environments, but officemates rely on others doing the job well and in a mutually supportive way. I advised teenagers that if they work hard when they are older, are easy to work with, and are responsible, they can achieve almost anything in the workplace. Very few employees bring that approach, and it's needed and appreciated.

Looking out for the other people we work with also makes a difference in office relationships. The new medical assistant in our office had to bring two-year-old twins and their parents to an exam room, weigh the children, check their heights, and administer and score a screening test. These toddlers were not happy with being brought to the room, and they did not want to be touched.

She was terrific with them and took care of all of her tasks. This took time, and she fell behind. She wanted to deliver the proper care to these children, but she also wanted to be timely. The fact that she fell far behind, coupled with her newness and desire to do well, devastated her, and I saw her crying.

When I had a chance, I told her that she had done an excellent job treating these children with care and kindness, which was precisely what she should have focused on. In my compliments, I tried to take away her self-criticism. I added that she didn't need to worry about falling behind since she was working with me. We would get through the rest of the day. If we were behind, that was fine; families would understand because I'm usually on time. I then told her that she wasn't scheduled correctly. She should not have had these twins without someone else being assigned to help. It wasn't her fault. I pointed out that she had done incredibly well under challenging circumstances.

I spoke this way because it was the simple truth and the right thing to do. She felt better and looked forward to working the next day. I don't know how this might affect who she is as a co-worker, boss, hospital CEO, mother, or whatever she does later in life, but such interactions make a difference; we feel better for taking such roles. Doing so combines our minds with our hearts. The workplace can also serve as a mirror for our self-development. If we don't work hard or aren't the boss or manager that other people want to work with, we can ask ourselves why and learn a lot.

Our Families

When Our Children Live at Home

Our heart's love is our greatest gift to our children. It fills them with strength, security, wholeness, and joy—all things they genuinely require. With our love central, and our trying to do our best for them, they can figure out how to overcome our mistakes without taking them personally. Working on ourselves is the greatest thing we can do for our children, as it helps us to keep love central in ourselves and our interactions.

The following meditation can help you align with love and motivate you to act from your best self. You can work through it once and repeat it as often as you find helpful. It can also be a part of your morning routine, and you can adjust it to include other people in your life. When you have a quiet time—before falling asleep or during prayer or meditation—picture your child and surround that child with love. You can use an image of the child in the present, as an infant, or any time in between. Work with this image until you see that the child feels your love and takes it in. With that established, reverse the process: picture your child's love for you and continue until you feel it.

If you have more than one child, work separately with each one. This inner work guides our relationships and directs our thoughts toward love. A second part of this meditation is to inwardly ask

what this child needs from you and what you have to offer them.

Raising Our Grown Children

Our grown children want our love and support. They neither want nor need our criticism. It was never helpful in the past, and now it is definitely not. You can stop criticizing every aspect of how they run their lives, including how they maintain their houses, raise their children, or their style. Take this beyond verbal criticisms; don't even have these negative opinions in your thoughts. Have a relationship instead. This can be very hard, but they will be glad for your efforts, and you will be, too.

You Are Your Parents' Child

". . . It's just like the fishing rod I gave you."

My mom and I were arguing when she said these words. I was married at the time, had two children, was a pediatrician, and she was referring to a fishing rod she'd gotten me when I was thirteen. Our parents will always see us as their children. To them, there's a straight line from when we were born until now. Though we've gone through changes and have reshaped ourselves and how we see and interact in the world, they might not see that. We don't have to prove ourselves and have them understand our views; these can be too entrenched for our parents to drop them. It's okay if they see you from a past perspective. See life through their eyes and work on what counts—your relationship.

Rain-Slicker Forgiveness

We can look past our differences using *rain-slicker forgiveness.* Chapter 2 reviewed four different kinds of forgiveness. This is the fifth. When I was a boy, I had a yellow, rubberized rain-slicker with metal clasps, a matching hat, and black boots. I could walk to school in downpours with it on, and rain did not penetrate this outer covering. Rain-slicker forgiveness allows the words, ideas, and behaviors of others that ordinarily bother us to roll off our backs. Compassion guides this. We forgive them for not understanding how their words and deeds might affect us. We can also forgive them for what sprang from their own difficult pasts. Working on healing ourselves develops compassion for the others who suffered, and we can show this by not holding them responsible for the thoughtless things they might say or for the filters through which they see us. There is a place where we need to stand firm, but that place is not in our relationships with our parents

Aging Parents

Parents who have been closed-minded or stubborn during their lives will not suddenly change when they age; don't expect them to mellow as they age. Instead, they might regularly complain about their lives and not take care of themselves as well as we would wish. Some won't take their medicines correctly or might not wear the alarms that ring if they fall. You can try to help them, but stop if they resist your help. Taking care of their health is not your role. You can voice your concerns with their physicians; otherwise, your aim should switch to having pleasant times with them. That's what they would like, and it's what you'll want to remember when their deaths do inevitably arrive.

Reflections

- If you don't regularly interact with appreciation toward the people who serve you, consciously try to do so for a few weeks. See if it makes a difference.
- Which of these relationship ideas seems most challenging for you to carry out?

Relationships We Choose

Casual friends

Casual friendships generally grow out of being together with someone a lot. These can be with our workmates, classmates, people who live near us, and friends of our friends. We aren't closer because something prevents that from happening. It could be our relationship's newness, their interests being different from ours, or something about them that bothers us. This kind of friendship can cause problems if we expect these friendships to be like those with our close friends. Here, we might have to avoid topics that bring discord, another variation on rain-slicker forgiveness.

Such a casual friend of mine was very opinionated, and I often felt baited into arguments with him. His staunch viewpoint did not allow an exchange of ideas, but I could usually manage not to fall into the trap of battling because we didn't speak to each other too often. With this infrequency, I could hold back. Then he moved into my town, and we saw each other more often. That became a problem, as avoiding arguments became harder. I valued our friendship but had to set boundaries; that meant seeing him less often. Setting boundaries is part of tending to a friendship.

Close Friends

Eric Jacobs lived next door to me. We were five years old, best friends, and we couldn't get enough of each other. Our apartments shared a mutual wall with a coat closet just beyond the entry door. To signal to each other that we were ready to go to school, we moved all the boots, coats, scarves, and everything else hanging in the closet and tapped on the inner wall.

Eric's family moved to Valley Stream, a suburban community about forty-five minutes away from our home when we were in third grade. My parents took me to visit him once, but his parents never brought him to visit. Our relationship ended; we never saw or spoke with each other again. Once Eric moved, I played with the other kids in my building and the neighborhood. I had fun, but it was not the same. I didn't have another close friendship until I was in college, though nothing in me had changed.

Close relationships are given to us, and I've seen this numerous times. Another example occurred when I was in graduate school. I went to Glacier National Park, and after setting up my tent, I saw a sign for a ranger-guided hike to Iceberg Lake. I rarely went on group hikes, but I decided to go. About twenty of us made the trip to this pristine glacial lake. The ranger informed us that a lake resembling Iceberg Lake could be seen by ascending to the top of the shale ledge before us. A woman my age and I decided to take the trip. A thunderstorm struck as we neared the top, and we hid under a shelf on the ledge. A few white mountain goats were grazing nearby. Afterward, we saw a rainbow stretching from Iceberg Lake to its sister lake. Mary and I are still close friends.

Wisdom plays a role in our most important relationships. We can relax and not worry. Not having a close romantic relationship does not necessarily mean there is something wrong with us. This free time allows us to develop other parts of ourselves. We can also inwardly ask if there is any meaning to our not having a close relationship or if there is any aspect of ourselves we should work on during this unattached time.

Intimate Relationships

Kristen came in for her seventeen-year-old wellness visit, and she looked happier than I'd seen her in a long time. I had been treating her for depression, and I wondered if my observation was accurate. I asked, and she and her mom agreed that she hadn't felt this good in years. I wondered why she felt better, and her answer was unexpected: "I dumped my boyfriend." She had been with him for two years and hadn't understood how much he had drained her.

He had a tough childhood, which played into his unpleasant behavior. He was short-tempered and mean. She felt this was due to his past and that her love could heal what hurt. Instead, though, she was sucked into his negativity. She'd fallen into the trap of thinking her love would be enough. That can happen, but the other person has to recognize they have a problem and appreciate your love for them despite their limitations.

I have told innumerable teenagers that taking on such projects doesn't work. We will fail if we think our love can fix someone without their interest in being fixed. Their past hurts will create barriers, destroy your relationship, and eventually erode your sense of well-being.

I surveyed divorced parents in my practice and asked if they were surprised they had gotten divorced if they looked back to how they felt when they first married. The vast majority said they weren't. The major exclusions occurred where one of them had an unexpected affair. I told teenagers about this and suggested that they avoid bad relationships. We often get warnings: if a relationship is one-sided— we like how they look, they like us, we are attracted to their social circle, or we like our intimate moments together—we should look more closely at the situation and leave it if we don't feel it's a good relationship. We can use this time to develop hobbies, enjoy our friends, and learn to spend time alone.

You deserve to be loved and appreciated. Your relationship won't turn out as you wish if you aren't respected and loved, no matter how long you stay or how hard you try. This is a reality and not a moral or ethical issue. See a professional if this is not a part of your intimate relationship.

Living with Someone: Creating Family Meetings

When we move in with our partners and spouses, we do so to enhance our lives. It's important to appreciate that we likely have different backgrounds, beliefs, and styles. We can hold family meetings to talk through these differences and reach common ground. We can discuss every aspect of living together during these meetings, including our approach to finances, household affairs, and raising children. We can also use them to evaluate our progress. Successful businesses meet regularly for similar planning and review sessions.

Andrea and I had very different views about child-rearing, but we weren't aware of this until we had children. Looking back, our differences made sense. We are very different people and come from very different family backgrounds. When our differences became a significant issue, we saw a psychologist, but the person we saw made our rifts bigger. It became clear that we'd split up if we didn't do something to change our trajectory.

We had to learn to talk to each other. We hired a babysitter to come to our house for a few hours on Sunday afternoons, and we went to a local pub armed with pens and paper. We began our family meetings by acknowledging and appreciating that we loved each other and our children. To solve problems, we needed to learn to hear and understand the other's perspective. With this, we could make plans. Our conversations also cut back on fights. If something upset us during the week, we could let it pass instead of blowing up, saving it as something to discuss at our Sunday meeting. After a while, we got good at talking to each other and could speak after the kids went to bed.

Sometimes, such meetings call for the involvement of a third party. If, for example, a couple cannot agree on their approach to spending, a financial planner could be called on for help.

These meetings aren't part of a date night nor a time for going out to have dinner together. They are meetings to discuss our most valued venture: our lives. I can't recommend them enough.

Marriage

Marriage (and solid partnerships) contain the potential for reaching a level of commitment I call *giving one's heart to the other*. Each person is solid in themselves and, at the same time, entrusts their life to the other. The two become one. Love marks their relationship as they each work toward inner growth and strive for their partner to also have the best possible life.

Reflections

- Where could you apply rain-slicker forgiveness in your life?
- How do you talk about differences with your partner or spouse?
- What do you think about the idea of giving your hearts to each other?

Loss, Breakups, and Death

Relationships also contain loss. The following are tips and thoughts that can be helpful.

Relationship Breakups

When the end of the relationship is your decision:

- **Trust yourself.** You decided to leave for a good reason. Pressure will likely be applied to change your mind. This especially happens if the other person is abusive. Be strong. If you need to get legal help or the police involved, then do that.

  The world can go topsy-turvy when a relationship ends. It can be hard to get your bearings when the other person ends the relationship, even if their deeds caused the end.

- Andrea and I were married for thirty years when our divorce became inevitable. Though my world was spinning, I had to serve my patients, think clearly, be present, and not have waves of overwhelming sadness, despair, and confusion flood me while I was working. I needed footholds to stand on, and I found them by returning to the building that burned down to discover its treasures. Three things helped me greatly:

1. We each acted in ways that made sense to us. Our actions were based on how we saw the world and what we'd learned from life. If she acted in ways that made sense to her, I couldn't fault her. This helped me to realize that things couldn't have been different. Little events didn't cause our breakup; it was due to fundamental aspects of who we were. This also helped me to let go of blaming her. How could I blame her for acting in ways she felt made sense?

2. When did I know this relationship wasn't right? I had to answer this question because I didn't want to follow the same pattern in future relationships.

3. Did I stay in the relationship longer than I should have? If so, why? Again, I wanted to avoid falling into that trap in the future.

A few thoughts about divorce if you have children:

- Keep your children out of your battles. They want to know that they have the best parents possible. Make peace on their behalf.

- Ensure the switch goes well when they go to the other parent's house. If there are issues to discuss, have that conversation before the exchange. Don't battle with the children present.

- Your households might be very different. One could be strict and demanding, and the other more laissez-faire. That's okay. Your children will figure it out. We did the same when we were in school. We had strict teachers and more laid-back ones, and we were able to sort out how to behave in each class.

- If your children are safe with the other parent, drop your worries and concerns. If you weren't different, you'd still be together.

- We don't have to be like the other spouse, and we don't need to compete with them. We want our children to feel comfortable and loved in both settings, and this is the greatest gift we can give them.

- When the kids switch houses, you might need to make adjustments. The receiving parent might need to be flexible. Going to a park, getting pizza, or playing on the living room floor can help with the transition.

- If you develop a serious relationship with another person, tell your children that you will never forget them and treat them accordingly. Set up times to go out with just your child. Children can feel lost, and it's up to you to head that off before that happens. This is especially important if your new partner has children or if you have children together. Don't let your own get lost. This doesn't mean you should favor them; just let them know you love them and that they are not alone.

- Discuss your connection to your child with your new partner. If they don't get it, reconsider the relationship. It's that important.

Death

These are a few points that I've learned from observing the lives of others who have lost a loved one:

- Feeling your world is upside down, in shock, and uncertain about everything is normal.
- The world protects us by giving us time to grieve. Trust yourself. Everyone grieves differently. Do what works for you.
- Some well-meaning people can try to help you, but that can make you feel worse. Remember that they love you, want to help, and don't know what to do.
- If you know that your loved one is okay—and people know this in various ways—take it to heart. Live with this. Let it ease your pain.
- As you start to heal, your love doesn't fade. You're only able to push away your pain for a while. It's like having a door that you can close only at certain times.
- There will be flashbacks. You may find yourself in an amusement park, beholding the joy of others, when you suddenly find yourself overcome with

uncontrollable tears as you reflect on the pleasant times you could have shared in that park. That's okay. Accept it. Embrace it. You can even enjoy the memories and talk to your loved one.

- Consider what your loved one would have wanted for you. They wouldn't want you to be miserable and suffer.
- You're free to enjoy yourself. Don't feel guilty.
- Some find benefit in joining bereavement or life-after-death groups with others who have suffered similar losses. If that's helpful, take advantage of these opportunities.

If children are involved:

- You are allowed to be sad and to cry. You don't have to protect them from your emotions. You're human, and they love you.
- Avoid saying anything from a religious standpoint that you don't fully believe. Saying "They are with God" or "God wanted them in heaven" is acceptable if you know this and have no doubt. But if that is not what you believe, don't try to sweeten reality by adding that. Be honest, say what you believe, don't say more. Your children will be able to find their way.
- They might need counseling. There are bereavement groups for children and teens.
- You can do fun things for a memorial. Go out to dinner and have your departed loved one's favorite

meal that you would have had with them, or go on an outing that they would have liked. Do all of this in their honor and memory. It allows your kids to honor their loved ones while also allowing them to be children.

- Let them know that they are free to enjoy themselves and laugh. That's absolutely what their loved one would've wanted.
- Most importantly, don't worry about being perfect. None of us are. Be you.

Prescription

- We hold the key to our relationships.
- We can take over the ownership of our lives.
- Our feelings enrich and expand our experience of life.
- Our emotions help us see where we are and where we want to go.

The next prescription discusses balance: the paradox of working hard while letting go of our intended outcomes as well as the 'work' of being happier.

PRESCRIPTION VI

Work Hard but Let Go of the Outcome

My daughter's fourth-grade orchestra played a slow-tempo piece for their year-end performance; each successive year, the piece they played was more complex. We grow from challenges; they push us to higher levels of accomplishment. We appreciate this in the sports, creative endeavors, and hobbies we enjoy. Life brings challenges, and this section teaches how to take them on successfully, grow, and remain fully ourselves.

This chapter adds depth to some of the topics covered in earlier chapters and includes fresh ideas that enhance our well-being, like making sound decisions and getting better sleep.

Opening to Love

Before I open my eyes in the morning, I connect with Love and let it fill my heart. If I wake with an alarm, I turn it off, close my eyes, and then fill myself with love. This grounds me, strengthens me, and sets my compass. You can enjoy its value independent of your background or feelings about yourself.

- Begin by remembering a time you felt loved. This could have been a powerful spiritual experience or a seemingly insignificant moment from long ago, such as petting your dog or a cat when you were a child or a grandparent making you something to eat. The event is not the issue; it's about capturing this feeling. A good time to work on this is right before falling asleep.

- Once you find this memory, let the events that brought the feeling fade; focus on the feeling it brought. Let this feeling gravitate toward your heart and radiate outward from there. Practice this during quiet times during your day, whether at work, home, in line at the supermarket, or while waiting for a traffic light to change. This exercise can also be done by remembering a prayer or verse that moves you. Hold the feeling it creates and let the words of the verse or prayer fade.

- After years of working with this, I no longer need to hold a memory. I pay attention to my heart and notice that it rotates slightly as it awakens, and a beam radiates from there outward.

Starting the day

After filling myself with Love, I keep my eyes closed and review my upcoming day. This review takes five to ten minutes and contains three parts: a cursory look at the details of the day ahead, a more detailed one, and then I consider *how I want to be* during my upcoming activities. This process helps me to prepare for the day ahead. A version of such preparation is routine whenever we care about an upcoming activity, whether in our professions, our athletic or creative endeavors, or when making plans for an important event. If thinking ahead helps, we can similarly use the idea to prepare for our upcoming day.

Benefits of These Daily Scans

I often remember details I might have forgotten when I go over my day, like taking a shopping list because I'll be going to the market after work or our child's friend is having dinner with us. In addition, stress drops when I see that I can get through the busiest parts of my day. It might also show me that I need to be a better planner, that I shouldn't take on so many activities, or that I need to rethink my kids' after-school commitments. When I encounter issues or ideas that need further thought, I can table them and think about them when I have more time.

The *how we want to be* review allows me to be myself, as in these examples:

- Our four-year-old daughter was rarely ready by the time we had to leave in the morning. We woke her early enough, but she still wasn't dressed for preschool on time. During my review, I appreciated that she wasn't ignoring us; she didn't have the developmental capacity to get dressed alone and got distracted. The morning I noticed this,

I went to her room to see how I could help and quickly realized that hovering wasn't the answer. I made a game out of getting ready: "You'd better not get your pajamas off before I get my socks on," and I made believe I was surprised and upset when she did. Then, I offered a new dressing challenge. We had fun, and she dressed painlessly. Once she was good at getting dressed, I could decrease my involvement, and she dressed easily and on her own.

- My child's schoolteacher had concerns, and we were meeting that evening. My feelings about this meeting were growing, and I knew it would be on my mind all day. During my morning review, I decided to manage my concerns about this meeting, similar to how I described working on emotions in that chapter. I considered the meeting a time for fact-gathering as if I were a reporter interviewing the teacher. I would listen and take notes but leave my emotions out of it. Later, when I had free time, I would think about what was said and consider my response. With the sting from the meeting removed, it wasn't on my mind during my day.

- I will be attending my children's soccer game, and their mom will be there with her new partner. I work with the family-gathering forgiveness described in Chapter Two and be welcoming and friendly. My children don't want to see anything else.

- I will think about how I can help our department's new pediatrician.

After my morning reviews, I again fill myself with Love. If my spouse is awake, we will surround each other with Love and do the same for our children and others. I am then ready for my day.

I also review what happened that day before I go to sleep. This is shorter, done in reverse, and grazes over highlights to see how my encounters went. Did I hold my emotional ground when I met with my child's teacher? How did I do with family-gathering forgiveness? Was I able to pull it off? If not, what triggered me, and what could I do differently the next time? This review is for me to learn and grow, not to be upset with myself.

My workday:

Setting Love as an Intention

After I parked my car at work, I'd close my eyes and ask Love to join me. I'd then go to my office, answer my most pressing messages and emails, and then visit my colleagues and coworkers to greet them, enjoy our connections, and review work-related issues. We are human beings trying to deliver the best care possible, and our personal interactions are an important part of the process.

Being Present and in the Moment

Before seeing patients, I review their charts, consider their current problems, and think about relevant issues I will want to discuss. When medical students were with me, I told them that part of our job is to give a present to each patient. When they looked puzzled, I explained that our present includes our caring, listening to their concerns, thinking about the issues they face, and offering a treatment plan with follow-up, all in a language they can understand. Before entering the room, I cleared my head of any personal issues and filled my mind with gladness for the person I was about to see. This human being entrusted their life to me; I looked forward to seeing them and wanted them to know I was there to serve them. I was ready, and so I stepped into the room.

The notion of focusing on patients who have a medical problem rather than simply treating the medical problem a patient has is an essential distinction. In fact, the Dartmouth medical students voted me the best teacher in pediatrics. I don't believe it was because my teaching was any better than anyone else's; I believe they appreciated being taught a humanized way to think about their patients.

I use the same approach in social interactions. Before meeting with someone, I take some quiet time to review their 'chart' and go over our past history. I look for topics we might want to discuss, and think about anything I know about that might interest them. Before unusually important or challenging conversations, I close my eyes and ask Love to join me. I've never had anything but wonderful conversations when I've asked Love to join me in this way.

Finding My Role at Work

Medicine was the perfect career for me because I could use my knowledge to help others live better lives. However, medicine can be a difficult field. Over half of the country's physicians experience job dissatisfaction, with physician burnout playing an increasingly powerful role in medicine. I experienced the same obstacles others faced and figured out how to manage them so I could focus my career on my personal interactions. This approach can help you thrive in your field, as well. The first step is to appreciate why you are there and what you want to achieve. Your job could be your dream job, a stepping stone to another career, or the only way you have to pay your bills. Appreciating this helps you assess your current situation and consider your next steps.

Contributing at work can make you feel valued, whether by providing excellent service to your customers or being a reliable, unflappable coworker—someone others can lean on. My work life taught me this, and I unconsciously learned this principle from my dad.

He came to this country in the 1920s and worked at a Western wear clothing factory packing boxes. Many of his fellow immigrants also held factory jobs until they left to develop their own careers. My dad couldn't. He was legally blind, unable to see the top E of an eye chart. He tried to become an independent patent attorney, as a law degree wasn't required back then, but he couldn't meet the reading and typing demands. He could only hunt a peck with his face on the keyboard, and a paper had to touch his nose for him to read it. He eventually gave up and continued at Halpern and Christenfeld, where he received his $100/week salary in $10 bills that were given to him in a small manilla envelope. He never complained about work or mentioned his long, ninety-minute bus and subway commute. When I was twelve, I once asked how work was. "Ah, they are so stupid," he replied, and his work life became instantly clear to me. His coworkers had less and less education as the years went by, and many didn't speak English.

My dad was 5'2" and very shy, so shy that I can barely remember his voice. I always felt that he had a heart of gold. A cousin worked with him one summer, and he told me something I didn't know: my dad had been elected shop foreman by his coworkers every year since he began working there. I am sure he said very little to them. I think his reliability, positive spirit, and overall goodness were noted, and we can all carry this attitude to our own workplaces.

If we decide to stay at our jobs, it's up to us to figure out how to step around the obstacles that could prevent us from being our best. As we do this, we will be more ourselves, be more filled with Love, and be more engaged with those we meet. We will feel like we contribute, and this will help us enjoy life more.

You might also need to find value outside of work and put your energy into it, whether through time with your family, friends, hobbies, or volunteer work.

Some work from home. Feeling vibrant comes with the challenge of staying fresh and energized despite having a lack of work-related social interactions. We need to know ourselves and know what works for us.

Parents caring for their kids at home have one of the most important jobs on the planet. The value and importance of this task are not always recognized. To counter the lack of prestige that can be experienced, I'd sometimes tell folks at home who are asked what they do for a living to say, "I head a research lab that focuses on developing a new generation of psychologically sound, caring, strong leaders."

The value and the challenge of this work must be fully appreciated by the parent who is earning a salary, and that salary must be seen as brought in by both parents. Family meetings are important to ensure that and to also look for ways to support the one at home. A neighbor, who was an architect, taught me the importance of this

His wife, also an architect, was home on maternity leave. One day, she mentioned that she had a headache. I was nearby and heard him respond, "That's probably because you didn't do anything all day." Wrong!

Forgiving in Our Closest Relationships

Forgiveness between close friends consists of discussing their disagreements to regain their appreciation of each other. This differs from the forgiveness that allows us to see past what would ordinarily be an obstacle to have a human connection. There can still be differences in politics, religion, or family life between close friends. One could be a sports enthusiast, and the other might not be interested, but they can maintain closeness and not focus where they don't have mutuality. Through our respect for each other, our caring for each other, and our enjoyment of our time together, we are friends.

Our close friends are a special group, and we commit to them. We can forgive them, but in a different way. If a friend doesn't call for a while or is late for an appointment, we know they didn't do this intentionally. If they start apologizing, we can tell them that friends don't need to apologize to each other; we know that their actions showed no disrespect or malice.

If they do something that hurts us, it is out of the usual bounds of our relationship and will make it difficult to let go without talking about it. That needs to be discussed. I went away with a few friends and a person I didn't know who was a friend of the other two. I did not feel well and couldn't join them in the planned activities. My friend, who is quite considerate, seemed to ignore me and did ask if I needed anything before they went out. I didn't mind their going out and leaving me behind. In fact, I encouraged it. It did bother me that he was not true to our relationship by seemingly ignoring me. This bothered me enough that I felt distance. I did not want that to happen to our friendship, so I spoke with him about it. He heard me and appreciated how I must have felt. That was the repair work we needed.

A medical school classmate, Hal Tobias, taught me another aspect of friendship. When someone said, "Hal, could you do me a favor?" before they said anything else, he answered, "Sure. What is it?"

Hal always followed through and did the favor. This impressed me so much that I took up the practice.

Forgiveness with Partners and Spouses

For our relationships as partners and spouses to work optimally, we must feel we are complete equals. Our views don't have to be identical, but we must be able to share them and know we will be heard, appreciated, and respected.

When there is a disagreement, we can hold a conversation to resolve the issue. Forgiveness means the relationship moves forward fully healed.

Setting Boundaries

Being able to say "no" is also critical to feeling good about ourselves; it's built into the very nature of our hearts and minds. Our expansive hearts bring the concerns of others to our consciousness, and we consider how we can offer our support. Our practical minds consider which relationships serve us and which need to be trimmed. A psychological puzzle demonstrates the need for setting limits: we feel good about ourselves when we help someone else, but helping others can also leave us feeling depleted, less energized, and used.

The difference between these two lies in how our efforts are received. If we are appreciated, whether through words or by sensing that we did the right thing, we feel good; if we feel our efforts are not valued or appreciated, we feel drained. We aren't helping anyone when we don't feel valued, underlining our need to cut back. We can't help everyone, and that's an inner reality.

When Relationships Don't Work

Sometimes, we want to be close to a group of friends or to a specific person, and we often take it personally if our friendship isn't accepted or the individual doesn't fall in love with us. We think this lack of acceptance is a sign of our having a shortcoming. If Wisdom is involved in our relationships, we see this differently. We can trust the outcome after checking to see if we aren't doing something that needs to be adjusted. Otherwise, to take this personally and blame ourselves would be like finding ourselves at fault if a piece of fruit lacks the sweetness we expected.

Progress Stemming from Our Inner Work

Working with Worries

I was driving into Boston and saw a large billboard advertising a plumber. I'd been enjoying the ride, but this sign suddenly made me think of our failing septic system. It likely had to be replaced, and replacing it would cost a lot. My stomach dropped, and I worried about paying for the septic system for much of the remaining drive. Had I been working on letting go of worry, I still might have felt a sinking feeling in my stomach on seeing the sign and remembering my septic system, but I would have soon realized, *Oh, this is a concern about money*, and I would have remembered that the Heavenly was my banker. If I were still worried, I'd use my time before falling asleep to think about how we'd pay for the septic system. I'd also go over my ideas about Wisdom and my finances. If I had seen that billboard after I had been working on my ideas about trust and money for a longer time, that billboard would not have tripped me up into thinking about my septic system, and I would have happily continued to enjoy the day. There's no reason for me to step out of my present moment because someone else installed an ad about their plumbing business.

Working Hard and Letting Go of Outcomes

Difficult emotions arise when we don't get what we want. We can feel frustrated, rejected, and all shades of associated experiences. Seen from a different angle, our drives, passions, desires, and interests make up who we are. The challenge is to learn from what the world is telling us. Are we after the wrong prize, do we need a fresh approach, or do we need to patiently watch the situation unfold and look for the hand of Wisdom? We will grow, be more effective, and we will be a better person for it if we do.

Aesop told a tale of a fox jumping to get a bunch of grapes from a vine that was out of reach. He couldn't get them and walked away, saying they were sour and that he really didn't want them. That is not the point here: it's about becoming wise.

Limiting Self-Blame

I opened my front door one morning and saw that I had left the trunk of my car open the night before. It had rained, and this open trunk pointed straight up. I wasn't the slightest bit upset with myself because I had been grappling with these ideas for a considerable amount of time. Blaming myself would not have created any worthwhile results; it wouldn't have encouraged me to exercise greater caution in the future, as I was already well aware of the importance of keeping my car trunk closed, and being generally upset would not have helped either. The only thought I took away was to air out the trunk when the rain stopped so it could dry without getting mildewy.

I took this a step further and realized that the same lack of blame would have been the only appropriate response if, instead of me, my partner, daughter, or friend had done the same.

Improving Sleep

Some people fall asleep easily and then wake up, and some have a hard time falling asleep. If you regularly don't sleep well, it's important to have a physical exam to be sure there are no underlying problems. Otherwise, working with your heart and mind can help with both of these.

Thinking is the reason we can't fall asleep, whether when first going to bed or upon waking during the night. To fall asleep, we have to let go of thinking, allow our consciousness to fade, and let our body's desire for sleep take over. Worries often spiral when we don't easily fall asleep; we think about everything that can go wrong. This furthers our wakefulness, and we don't have a way to break the cycle.

Use this time for inner work. Instead of worrying, fill yourself with Light and Love. Work on healing childhood hurts, filling yourself with Love, or on healing any current concern. Substituting inner work for random worries is an excellent use of time. When you get tired, go to sleep.

Some people who have difficulty sleeping worry that they won't get enough sleep. This worry builds up and prevents them from being able to sleep. Heart and mind can help with sleeping: lie on your back, get comfortable, put your hands near the bottom of your ribs, and say a short prayer, mantra, or words of 'thank you.' You can softly repeat, *Thank you, God;*, *Love is my center;* or *I live in Love*. This relaxes your body, slows your breathing, and this relaxed state is as good as sleeping. In the morning, you will notice that you are refreshed; you will also notice that you did sleep. If I can't fall asleep, or if I wake up, I no longer worry. In addition, I've also used this time to work through issues on my mind, and I've found this to be very helpful.

Three-to-five-Minute Naps

A three-to-five-minute nap can be remarkably refreshing. I find a comfortable spot—this can be as basic as sitting with my feet on my desk and leaning my head against a wall. I set my alarm for this short time and close my eyes. The alarm guards against my taking too long and reassures me that I can afford these few moments of quiet. I keep an airplane pillow in my car for such naps. Please note that these short naps don't replace a bad night's sleep. Staying in the moment, listening, and being in the zone takes mental energy. These short bursts of rest help you to recharge. I commonly have deep, dreaming sleep during these naps. If I don't fall asleep, they are still refreshing and revitalizing, like a restorative shower.

Some people automatically reject the idea of napping,

saying it makes them groggy. This kind of nap doesn't do that. Try it. You have nothing to lose.

Decision-Making without Regret

Making good decisions contributes to happiness. The key to making good decisions is appreciating that we can't make bad ones. We don't have to look back and think we could have made a better decision. That's judging from where we are now, and it has nothing to do with the circumstances when we made the decision. Life is about growth and constant learning. At times, nothing is more helpful than being in a situation we don't want to be in, because we can use that to inspire us to make needed changes.

Some practical approaches can help with decision-making, and I've listed a few here that I've built into my own life.

- Some daily decisions are small, and these are plentiful. We have to make them, and we often don't have much time. Remember, you want to do the right thing. That will guide you. I often add, "Dear God, this is the choice that I am making. Please hit me over the head if I should do this differently." With this, I know I am doing my best and can leave fear behind.
- Sometimes, important decisions affect our lives and no one else's. Here, our task is to listen within, explore the reasons behind our decision, and look at the possible downsides. We are done if we can see that we will be fine if our plan doesn't work

as we hoped. We don't have to get the opinions of others. Those opinions can even be unhelpful because someone else doesn't see the situation as we do. We can't lose. We have our plan, and the plan includes how we will go forward if things don't work out as we wish.

- Sometimes, we have to make decisions when things aren't so clear. One friend suggested a seven-day method for making such decisions: wake up for three mornings and consider that you decided to go one way. See how it feels while looking at the details. Then, wake up for three mornings and picture that you made the other choice. Again, imagine how this choice plays out. On the seventh morning, weigh the pros and cons of each and choose.
- We could examine our decision-making process to see if we missed something that we don't want to repeat in the future.
- We are where we are, and we are never alone. Love and Wisdom are always with us.

Asking for Higher Guidance

I learned about asking for guidance from Julie Pierce. I had given her a ride home from a friend's house, and during the two-and-a-half-hour trip, she told me about her practice of asking for Higher Guidance and that she never makes a decision without asking first. I'd never heard of this and was fascinated. I visited her the next day to learn more, and she came to our house the following weekend so that Andrea could also speak with her.

Now, this idea makes so much sense to me, and it is built into my life. If Love lives within and its Wisdom works through our lives, it's impossible that we can't have a two-way conversation when we are stuck. This is not about asking for something we want, like a job or a raise. It's asking what to do.

Since this idea was new to me, I will assume it might also be new to you. I will explain four different ways I have used the process of asking for Higher Guidance.

- My daughters were teenagers, Andrea was working late, and the three of us were going to have dinner together. They are wonderful people, and I love them dearly, but something they said bothered me. I thought I was overreacting, but I was really bothered by it. I thought a run would get my upset out of my system, so I asked them to get dinner ready and went out for a jog.

  When I returned to the house, I was surprised to notice my feelings had not dissipated. I wasn't sure if I should make this an issue at the table or drop it, so I got quiet and asked for Higher Guidance before entering the house. I heard that I should drop it, so I completely let go of my upset. We had the most delightfully wonderful dinner. Several days later, I reviewed my thoughts about what happened with them. It was really minor; I addressed it with them, and it quickly resolved. I was so glad that I asked for guidance. I don't think I would have come up with that on my own.

- I was a part of a book club that met via Zoom, and I only knew one person directly, the group leader. Toward the end of one session, one member of the group said something directed toward me, "You're always talking about love," and her words were said as a criticism.

  I was upset and felt like I wasn't valued, heard, or appreciated. This occurred at the very end of our meeting, and I wasn't sure about what to do. I didn't want to stay in a group that didn't value ideas that I cherished. If the meeting had been in person, I could have stayed behind and talked to the person who made that statement. I decided to write a letter to the man who headed our group, telling him what happened, and asking his opinion on what to do, and this included the possibility of my dropping out.

  My feelings reminded me of an incident that the former headmaster at the Garden City Waldorf school, John Gardner, once told me he faced. I decided to ask him, though he was no longer living. Before going to sleep that night, I asked whether to write this note. I had a dream. I was seated in a large auditorium before a concert. I turned around, and to the right of me, in a row behind me, John Gardner was about to sit. He looked like the man

I knew when I was a schoolteacher. He greeted me with a warm smile, and we shook hands.

When I woke up, I had no doubt that this dream was an affirmation that I should write the letter. I got out of bed and wrote for about three hours. When I thought I had the right tone, I felt John's presence with me again, and I knew it was ready.

I sent the note to the head of our group, and he wrote back, saying I shouldn't worry and that it wasn't a big deal. He suggested that I stay and added that my presence in the group was appreciated. I felt he'd heard me, and I trusted his response. A few weeks later, I initiated a conversation in the group that was similar to the one that prompted my groupmate's comments. This time, the same woman thanked me for bringing up my points, saying they were very helpful. No one had told her about my earlier frustration or my letter. I felt at home in the group and was glad I had worked through my concerns.

• I was working on an earlier version of this book, and one chapter was going to be titled *Know Thyself*. I wasn't clear about what I wanted to say and took a long walk on a beautiful dirt road in rural Vermont to think through the chapter. At the end of the walk, I felt I hadn't made a lot of progress and was discouraged. I inwardly asked if I should continue with this project, feeling I needed support to go on.

I passed a movie theater in a small town on my way home. I had never heard of the movie that was playing, but I decided to go. It was set in Greece. At one point, the multigenerational family that the film was about was sitting on a patio, enjoying a meal, overlooking the green, spacious, and hilly countryside. The family patriarch stood and made a toast, "May we follow in the footsteps of the ancient ones and remember their most important suggestion: *Know Thyself.*"

My hair stood on edge, and I felt chills along my arms. Though I couldn't figure out how, I knew this was for me to hear. I felt encouraged and knew I should go on with writing the chapter.

- We can also ask about our finances. Andrea and I were living in a farmhouse on a large parcel of land built in the early 1800s. We hadn't expected it, but the house was a money drain. We paid more than we should have and put a lot of money into it, but it still needed more. We were debt-heavy. Selling the house would leave us still owing a lot. We were more than broke. When a piece of mail unexpectedly announced that the credit limit on one of our cards was extended by $5,000, we were overjoyed with the extra money we suddenly had. We were desperate and didn't know what to do. We'd made mistakes and didn't know how to go forward.

  We asked for guidance together. After getting quiet, sharing our love, and sharing our confusion, we asked what to do. An image came to me of a forester who had once come out to our land to see if there would be any money in doing a limited, selective tree harvest. We had decided against it, and I hadn't thought about him again. When I saw his picture in my mind's eye, I called him. He told me that he had retired and then gave me the name and number of someone who had taken his place. I called this person, and he told me that he would come out to walk the land with me.

During our walk, he asked if we had a conservation easement. I didn't know what that meant, and he told me that New Hampshire offered such easements to preserve the landscape. Instead of the state owning lands, interested land owners received money for their promise not to develop that land, now or in the future. The owners were given the money they'd have received for developing the land, and this agreement stayed with the land independent of ownership.

The next day, I went to our town offices and was told that the town had just approved a large sum of money for conservation easements at its annual meeting the week before. We applied, got an easement, and were paid enough to settle our accounts and have some money left over. This would never have happened had we not asked for guidance.

In my experience, asking for guidance doesn't necessarily mean hearing a specific answer; it can be a feeling or a thought when listening to a song. It's something that shakes you, and you know that this is an answer to what you asked.

Andrea had stayed in our old house after our divorce. One day, she asked if I could help her put the storm windows on the screened-in porch. These were full-length, and I had always taken care of them. I said I would, but I certainly felt funny going over there. No matter how much we had said that we would stay friends, this was difficult for me. I asked for support. As I drove around the corner and onto her street, the Beatles sang on the radio, "*I was alone, I took a ride. I didn't know what I would find there.*" Goosebumps again. I can't say how this happens, but it does.

I write about asking for guidance because it has been a very helpful discovery, one I hadn't known about. It has never failed me. I would have dropped it as a tool if it had not stood up to this test. I don't ask flippant questions in a willy-nilly way. I ask when I sincerely want insight into the right thing to do—when I'm just not sure. How could the Wisdom and Love in my life not help me if I asked that way?

The Work of Being Happier

Being happier takes work, but it's not the kind of work that has negative connotations; it's the work we undertake when we want to improve our skills, whether in our hobbies, creative activities, or professional endeavors. It doesn't feel like work because we grow from it. To be in flow, for example, we put all of our attention into our task, and we lose ourselves in the activity. That's where its joy lies. If we didn't think happiness took work, it would mean that happiness was given to us on a platter. That occurs sometimes and with some things, but that's clearly not the rule. The following two stories show this 'work of happiness' from two very different directions.

I spent a rare day off writing at the Boston Atheneum (a Boston library), had dinner at a favorite restaurant, and went to get my car from the garage under the Boston Common. When I started the car, a spark shot out from under the hood, and the engine didn't turn on again. I called my insurance company, and they were sending a tow truck. I thought I would have it towed to a VW dealership some twenty miles to the north, in the direction of my house, and stay overnight at a nearby hotel. I would get a loaner car from the dealership and use it until my car was ready. I called several hotels near that dealership, and there were no rooms.

At the same time, the tow truck driver called to tell me they weren't coming for me. The underground garage had a low ceiling. Their tow truck wouldn't fit. I found out that the garage had a special fleet of trucks for this purpose, and its crew only worked during the daytime. I'd have to stay in Boston and get towed in the morning. Luckily, I didn't have to start seeing patients that next day until 1:00 PM, so I could still get to my office on time if I stayed in town and got the car towed in the morning. I opened my laptop to book a hotel room and discovered that the entire city of Boston was filled; there were no rooms at any price. The Red Sox were in town, Adele was giving a concert, and Bruce Springsteen was also performing nearby.

The driver of another tow truck called me. He said that he and his friend, who also had a tow truck, would meet me outside the garage at 11:15 p.m.. Their vehicles weren't the right height, but they wanted to try and get me out. These two drivers had great enthusiasm, and we pushed my car to the taller entry vestibule. This wasn't easy, as the power steering was out, but we did it. We got the car onto one of the trucks, and they towed it to the dealership near my house. Afterward, the driver kindly drove me home. I closed my front door at 2:30 a.m.

The local VW dealership sent a car to pick me up the next morning. The battery had shorted out. The repair was considered a wear-related issue, and it wasn't covered by my extended warranty. I had to pay the $750 for the towing, tips, and the battery.

I tell this story because I did not let upset enter my thinking at any step along the way, not at all. Not only wouldn't it have helped, but getting frustrated could have been an impediment. I'm not sure the drivers would have done the extra work of pushing my car out of the garage had I been upset instead of appreciative. I'd kept the driver company and chatted the whole way during the late-night journey, and the cab was cold, noisy, and drafty. I wanted to make sure he didn't fall asleep during the ninety-minute trip. We had a fun drive, and I thought the good mood we developed was the reason he agreed to take me to my house, which was a few miles further. I slept well that night without angry thoughts about the evening spinning around in my head. I was grateful that the dealership took care of my car so quickly and pleased that they sent someone to pick me up. I blocked any dismay about the cost, and I was fresh and ready for my first patient. I acted as if nothing unusual had happened in the previous twelve hours. They did not need my problems to be a part of their medical visit.

When I was in my late forties, I decided to thank my mom for all she had done for me. She had her quirks, but I realized she had done her best. I think this idea came from my appreciation of all the parents I'd seen in my practice. Just saying 'Thank You' to her wouldn't get my point across. Giving her a present wouldn't work, either. Her adage always was: *Don't just tell me how you feel; show me by the way you act.* I realized that my only possible route was to let her know that she raised a nice kid, and that meant I had to stop arguing with her—about anything. My upset never changed her, so I decided to commit myself to this new approach.

Toward the end of her life, I convinced her to move to New Hampshire, where I lived, and I found an assisted living facility for her that was close to my house. I went out to dinner with her weekly. She regularly pushed one of my pet peeves when we ate out. After we each studied the menu, ordered our meals, and the food was brought to our table, she'd look at mine, and ask if she could taste it.

"Mom," I would say, "we just got our food. Enjoy what you ordered. You can certainly have some of mine, but let's enjoy what we each ordered first."

My new approach meant ignoring this former trigger without getting flustered in the least.

A few years later, she moved into a nursing home near my office. I visited her at lunchtime, and we ate together. That first day, she looked at my lunch and talked about how good it looked. I just gave her what I had. She could not let the nursing home lunch remain uneaten, and it became my lunch. From then on, I prepared food I knew she would like, gave that to her, and I had the lunch the nursing home provided. Let me just say that this was not a gourmet eating destination, and I ate my lunch without a hint of being anything but delighted.

During one visit, my mom pointed to the handheld buzzer for calling the nurse. Smiling, she said, " I figured out that yelling for the nurse works much better than this buzzer."

This was despite her having an ill roommate. Instead of being upset, I just said, "Mom, you are so wonderfully unique. I don't think anyone else could have come up with that idea," and I chuckled.

I also became friendly with the staff and spent time chatting with them before and after visiting my mom to make sure they were doing okay. They enjoyed her and liked her spunk.

Without our arguing, we developed a remarkable closeness. When I arrived, we created a routine: we hugged each other, but we each took off our glasses before hugging. When

I bent down to her wheelchair, our glasses-less hug allowed our faces to press together, and I felt an indescribable energy from her: it was a mother's pure love for her son. I was so fortunate to have experienced this. Tears came to my eyes when I first wrote this.

Toward the end, she was in a coma, and I sat by her side, singing softly to her as she took her last breath. My decision not to argue with her led to outcomes I could not have imagined.

FINAL PRESCRIPTION
Epilogue

We started with the idea that full human thinking includes our hearts as well as our minds. As we think with our hearts, we experience another person's perspective, imagine their problems through their eyes, and then ask how we can best support them. Love lives within, and as we work with it, we feel strengthened, solid, and we are ourselves.

We explored various issues that get in the way of our feeling that Love. The most notable of these are our childhood hurts. We learned to tackle these hurts through Focused Inner Listening. Our pain doesn't instantly disappear, but as we let light enter, our inner wounds lighten, as well as the problems that stemmed from them. With these splinters removed, we are increasingly ourselves. The Love Within, or whatever term one uses for that Higher Deity, is also wise, for Love and Wisdom are one and the same thing. Our lives are permeated with Love and Wisdom, and we can use them to eliminate worries from our lives and align our emotions with our highest selves. With Love in our hearts, we not only meet life's challenges; we become part of a greater healing.

As a physician, I've been impressed with how certain ventures capture the interest of a wide swath of scientists at certain times. Modern medicine took great strides in the early 1900s; inventors from around the world worked on the idea of a personal computer when Steve Jobs, Steve Wozniak, and Bill Gates offered their versions to the public; while currently, many are working on artificial intelligence.

I now see that this is a time to switch our thinking to include the heart as an equal to the mind. Each individual's effort at thinking with heart and mind opens the space for others to do the same, even people we don't know. This improves our quality of life and enhances the health of the world. Being bigger hearted is a prescription for the healing and connection the world so desperately needs.

If these pages resonate, you are invited to continue the conversation at my website, Biggerhearted.com. There, you can ask questions, sign up for newsletters, participate in workshops, and request one-on-one work to further your work with these ideas.

ADDENDUM

Meditations on Being Bigger Hearted

The Heart's Love

Love opens a door that allows you to see through the eyes of another. From this perspective, you can inwardly ask how to give them your support.

Love is a spiritual path.

The heart's love strengthens, heals, and uplifts. Compassion and gratefulness radiate from the heart.

Material experience can limit one's ability to be happy, but when the heart is included, happiness becomes limitless.

The heart allows you to find yourself, experience another, and assess your actions.

Healing Childhood Hurts

The process of healing begins by replacing the idea that you were at fault for your difficult childhood settings and appreciating that the bad things said about you weren't true.

Those who hurt you acted through their own hurts. It is time to end the cycle.

You can fill yourself with love, even if you missed feeling loved as a child. Love is an objective, transcendent reality. You can open to it and let it in.

Rebuilding starts with loving yourself and forgiving yourself for all that's happened since childhood. You can turn it around.

Focused Inner Listening provides a workspace for going forward.

You can let go of blaming those who hurt you. You don't have to fix them; you don't have to be close to them, and you can still forgive them.

Letting Go of Worry

Worries don't bring change.

Worrying takes you out of the present and clouds how you see the world.

You can be present, see clearly, and make the best choices when you are without worry.

If you see that you could manage the reasonably worst possible outcome, you don't need to worry. It's like knowing the future and being okay with it.

You are not alone; Love and Wisdom are always present.

Feeling and Emotions

—Self-doubt

Wisdom created your strengths and your shortcomings. You grow through them.

Life wouldn't be real if you were faultless.

Don't use intellectual standards to judge your heart-based efforts. They have different origins, aims, and purposes. Using the wrong assessment tool can create unnecessary self-doubt.

Appreciate that life is about learning and growing. Don't take criticism, or even failure, personally.

—Guilt

If the rules handed down from higher authorities—your parents, those you respect, or religious and spiritual traditions—are not yours, you don't need to follow them. Follow what makes sense to you at any given time.

When you are true to yourself, you do not run counter to any true spiritual or life-affirming path.

—Feelings

Feelings are natural instincts, such as feeling cold or hungry. As human beings, we can go beyond our basic instincts to care for the betterment of ourselves and others.

—*Emotions*

You can also adjust your emotional responses instead of acting instinctively. When you are angry, frustrated, or loss of control, you can consider the cause of your reaction, think about your response, and develop actions that allow you to go forward genuinely, freely, and as yourself.

Relationships

To develop solid, intimate relationships:

- Don't try to fix someone who doesn't ask to be fixed. Skip bad relationships. Engage in other activities instead.
- Enhancing your life is the only reason to choose to live with another person. If you don't think a relationship will do that, back off. Trust your instincts.
- Family meetings can help you and your partner get onto the same page.

- Two become one when you and your partner decide to give your hearts to each other.

Relationships end because each sees life differently and acts accordingly.

Study the lessons of failed relationships before entering new ones.

You deserve to be treated well; treat the one you love the same way.

Work hard and let go of outcomes:
Set love as the intention for your day.

Fill yourself with love in the morning and before going to sleep.

Review the upcoming day before rising, and review the day that has passed before falling asleep.

ACKNOWLEDGEMENTS

This book was a process, and I would like to thank my many friends who helped along the way. Some particularly stand out: my sister Marilyn for her unending support and challenging questions; my cousins and lifelong friends, Steven Schneebaum and Michael Shpizner, who were not only critical sounding boards but also helpful early editors; Jeff and Janet Kane, Jack Petrash, Nancy Reuben, and Julie Pierce who listened to me for hours and offered insightful feedback as I grappled with my ideas, and Pam Rainey, John Tomlinson, and Bill Rider, early readers whose helpful encouragement was so appreciated.

I was remarkably fortunate to find professionals who helped with the actual writing of this book. Jennifer Repo and Jacquelyn Mitchard provided patience, guidance, and needed editorial help, and without the many members of the Steve Harrison/Jack Canfield Team, this book would never have reached its final form. I'm particularly grateful to Cristina Smith and Jeffrey Berwind for their insightful suggestions and encouragement and to Christy Day for putting it together.

About the Author

Ron Schneebaum, MD, a pediatrician who was in practice for 40 years, a Diplomate of the American Board of Pediatrics, and a fellow of the American Academy of Pediatrics, also served on the clinical faculty of Dartmouth College's Geisel School of Medicine, where he established a program, *Fresh Perspectives*, to help children and teens with behavioral, psychological, emotional, and school issues. The Dartmouth medical students he taught voted him Best Teacher in Pediatrics. After a career of helping the patients and families he saw live better lives, he retired from clinical practice to teach a larger audience what he learned about happiness, living fully, and being ourselves.

Dr. Schneebaum has two adult daughters, and his hobbies include organic gardening, hiking, woodworking, photography, and cooking.

www.ingramcontent.com/pod-product-compliance
Lightning Source LLC
Chambersburg PA
CBHW071433130726
47997CB00006B/2061